UNSEEN POETRY

AN AQA ESSAY WRITING GUIDE

AUTHOR: HUGH FOLEY
SERIES EDITOR: R. P. DAVIS

First published in 2021 by Accolade Tuition Ltd
71-75 Shelton Street
Covent Garden
London WC2H 9JQ
www.accoladetuition.com
info@accoladetuition.com

ISBN 978-1-913988-08-1

FIRST EDITION
1 3 5 7 9 10 8 6 4 2

CONTENTS

EDITOR'S FOREWORD

In the unseen poetry portion of your GCSE English Literature exam, you will be presented with two questions plus two poems that share a common subject. The first question (worth 24 marks) will be exclusively about the first of the two poems, and will ask you to discuss how a particular aspect of the poem is presented. The second question (worth 8 marks) will ask you to compare the first and second poem, and to discuss how the poets present their common subject in a different or not so different way.

Naturally enough, the first question – the one worth 24 marks – will be your top priority. Of course, there are many methods one might use to tackle a question of this kind. However, there is one particular technique which, due to its sophistication, most readily allows students to unlock the highest marks: namely, **the thematic method.**

To be clear, this study guide is not intended to explain everything you need to know about poetry: there are many great guides out there that attempt to do just that. No, this guide, by sifting through a series of mock exam questions, will demonstrate how to organise a response thematically and thus write a stellar essay: a skill we believe no other study guide adequately covers! I have encountered students who have structured their essays all sorts of ways: some by writing about the poem line by line, others by identifying various language techniques and giving each its own paragraph. The method I'm advocating, on the other hand, involves picking out three to four themes that will allow you to holistically answer the first question: these three to four themes will become the three to four content paragraphs of your essay, cushioned between a brief introduction and conclusion. Ideally, the themes will follow from one to the next to create a flowing argument. Within each of these thematic paragraphs, you can then ensure you are jumping through the mark scheme's hoops.

A statue of the Ancient Greek poet Homer: the author of *The Odyssey* and *The Iliad*, and generally considered the granddaddy of Western poetry!

So to break things down further, each thematic paragraph will include various point-scoring components. In each paragraph, you will quote from the poem, offer analyses of these quotations, then discuss how the specific language techniques you have identified illustrate the theme you're discussing. Don't worry if this all feels daunting. Throughout this guide, Hugh (the talented author!) will be illustrating in great detail – by means of examples – how to build an essay of this kind.

(For the shorter second question – the 8 marker – Hugh will also be showing you how to pick one interesting point of comparison, and to explain how this thematic difference or similarity is achieved by the poets' language).

In your exam, both poems are likely to be *about* some general subject or topic: the weather, grief, music, beaches, prophecy, etc. But the poems' **themes,** the things you are trying to describe in your answer, are going to be closer to the different things the poem says about the weather, grief, music, beaches, etc. The poem will normally offer you a sort of argument or story: the unfolding of more than one idea about what the weather, grief, music, beaches etc. *mean* to the poet, or the speaker, or to us all. So beaches might first make us happy to escape from work or school, and then make us feel sad as we realise we have to return to our everyday life, but also leave us refreshed. If these are the three ideas we get about beaches from the poem, these could be our themes, and each paragraph is then going to explain why you think that this theme is what the poem has to say about beaches, and how the language helps to make the point.

The beauty of the thematic approach is that, once you have your themes, you suddenly have a direction and a trajectory, and this makes essay writing a whole lot easier. However, it must also be noted that extracting themes in the first place is something students often find tricky. I have come across many candidates who understand the techniques a poem might use inside and out; but when they are presented with a question under exam conditions, and the pressure kicks in, they find it tough to break their response down into themes. The fact of the matter is: the process is a creative one and the best themes require a bit of imagination.

In this guide, Hugh will take eight exam-style unseen poetry papers – each containing two questions and two poems – and will put together a plan for each and every question: a plan that illustrates in detail how to satisfy the mark scheme's criteria. Please do keep in mind that, when operating under timed conditions, your plans will necessarily be less detailed than those that appear in this volume.

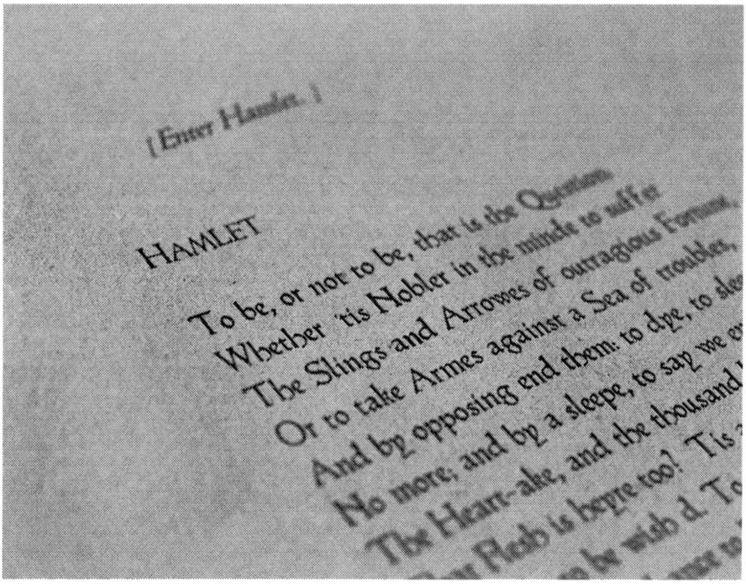

Shakespeare's 'To be or not to be' speech from *Hamlet*, perhaps the most famous lines of poetry in the English language.

Before I hand you over to Hugh, I believe it to be worthwhile to run through the two Assessment Objectives the exam board want you to cover in your response to this section of the exam – if only to demonstrate how effective the thematic response can be. I would argue that the first Assessment Objective (AO1) – the one that wants candidates to 'read, understand and respond to texts' and which is worth 12 of the total 24 marks up for grabs in the first question – will be wholly satisfied by selecting strong themes, then fleshing them out with quotations. Indeed, when it comes to identifying the top scoring candidates for

AO1, the mark scheme explicitly tells examiners to look for a 'critical, exploratory... conceptualised' response, supported by 'judicious references' – the word 'concept' is a synonym of theme, and 'judicious references' simply refers to quotations that appropriately support the theme you've chosen.

The second Assessment Objective (AO2) – which is also responsible for 12 marks in the first question – asks students to 'analyse the language, form and structure used by a writer to create meanings and effects, using relevant subject terminology where appropriate.' As noted, you will already be quoting from the poem as you back up your themes, and it is a natural progression to then analyse the language techniques used. In fact, this is far more effective than simply observing language techniques (personification here, alliteration there), because by discussing how the language techniques relate to and shape the theme, you will also be demonstrating how the writer 'create[s] meanings and effects.' Now, in my experience, language analysis is the most important element of AO2 – perhaps 8 of the 12 marks will go towards language analysis. You will also notice, however, that AO2 asks students to comment on 'form and structure.' Again, the thematic approach has your back – because though simply jamming in a point on form or structure will feel jarring, when you bring these points up while discussing a theme, as a means to further a thematic argument, you will again organically be discussing the way it 'create[s] meanings and effects.'

You'd be surprised how cheaply you can get hold of poetry these days!

My (and Hugh's) hope is that this book, by demonstrating how to tease out themes from a poem, will help you feel more confident in doing so yourself. I believe it is also worth mentioning that the themes Hugh has picked out are by no means definitive. Asked the very same question, someone else may pick out different themes, and write an answer that is just as good (if not better!). Obviously the exam is not likely to be fun – my memory of them is pretty much the exact opposite. But still, this is one of the very few chances you will get at GCSE level to actually be creative. And to my mind at least, that was always more enjoyable – if enjoyable is the right word – than simply demonstrating that I had memorised loads of facts.

PAPER ONE: POEMS ON PAINTINGS

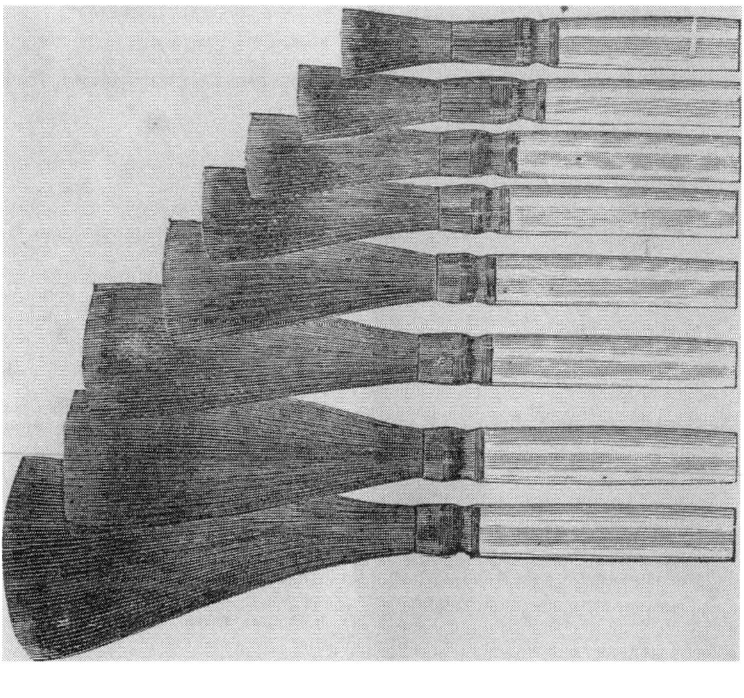

ESSAY PLAN: CHRISTINA ROSSETTI'S 'IN AN ARTIST'S STUDIO'

In an Artist's Studio
Christina Rossetti

One face looks out from all his canvases,
One selfsame figure sits or walks or leans:
We found her hidden just behind those screens,
That mirror gave back all her loveliness.
A queen in opal or in ruby dress,
A nameless girl in freshest summer-greens,
A saint, an angel — every canvas means
The same one meaning, neither more or less.
He feeds upon her face by day and night,
And she with true kind eyes looks back on him,
Fair as the moon and joyful as the light:
Not wan with waiting, not with sorrow dim;
Not as she is, but was when hope shone bright;
Not as she is, but as she fills his dream.

*opal – a jewel that shines in multiple colours
*wan – thin or weak

Q1. In 'In an Artist's Studio,' how does the poet present the artist's work?

[24 marks]

Before we dive in...

In this first plan, I will go into a little more detail about how we look for the material to turn into our answer. We have a subject, 'art', but we need to find some themes. Remember: we have two assessment objectives, AO1 (our understanding of what the poem is saying), and AO2 (our ability to see how language, form and structure create meaning).

In order to meet these two objectives, each paragraph will have to make our thematic point. That is to say, tell us something about what the poem means. We will then support this point with quotations. We have to analyse quotations in one of two ways. The first is to explain how it means what we say it means, and the second is to show us how the language or structure helps to strengthen that meaning, or even to create it. These two analyses are not always totally separable, but I will try to highlight how my answer manages to do both.

Think of the way language creates meaning in a poem like this: when I talk, it is not just the words I am saying that create my meaning. It is also my tone of voice, or even how loud I am saying it. In a poem on the page, a writer has to find other ways to create these effects. She is not in the room with you. She may try to create patterns using written language that do something similar. A repeated sound can make a written sentence more like a shout, or it can make it more like a whisper, or like sarcasm. A particular metaphor can bring in a different mood. If I say you are beautiful like a polished stone,

I'm not just bringing the beauty into the meaning, but other aspects of the stone—perhaps its hardness or coldness. Beautiful like a stone is different from beautiful like a rainbow. Try, when you read, to think about what kind of tone the writer is creating.

So, let's look at this poem, and think about some questions that we might ask ourselves to get started on our plan. Are there moments where it is harder or easier to understand? Are there recurring images? How do these change what we think the poem is saying? What words are repeated? Do we recognize the pattern or form of the poem?

I'll answer that last question briefly, because it may help us with our plan. This poem is a Petrarchan sonnet, so you might recognize that pattern from Elizabeth Barrett Browning's 'Sonnet 29', if you did *Love and Relationships*. 'Ozymandias', by Percy Shelley, from *Power and Conflict* is also a sonnet, but the pattern of rhymes is slightly different.

A sonnet, you might remember, is a 14-line rhyming poem, normally in **iambic pentameter**.[1] However, these features are not important by themselves. If the poem is in iambic pentameter that only matters if you can tell me that the iambic pentameter is doing something to make the poem meaningful. Why has Rossetti told us what she wants to tell us in a sonnet? The same question holds true of all AO2 language features. Why has the poet used them? To get the top marks, you have to connect the features (plausibly) to a purpose. This is why we are looking for themes. We want our themes to be supported by the language features. **We do not want to make a list of techniques**.

The key question then is how do any patterns we notice change our understanding of the themes? In the answer below, I will try to show you how we might plan to answer that question.

Introduction

In our introduction, we want to begin with a small summary of what we think is happening in the poem and the themes that we are going to cover. It is not strictly necessary to mirror back the exam question, but it almost always helps to focus your answer. Notice, in our little introduction we have met AO1, and have found a particularly 'judicious' quotation at the end – something that encapsulates our interpretation of the poem. We will need to do a bit more in order to meet AO2, but the introduction should already show the examiner that we mean business.

> "In the poem 'In an Artist's Studio', Christina Rossetti presents the artist's work as fixated on a single woman. Her image recurs throughout his paintings in different guises, but Rossetti makes this fixation disturbing. As we proceed through the poem, we come to realise that the woman in the paintings is transformed into an object, 'not as she is, but as she fills his dream'. What is disturbing about this is that, even though his art has the power to compensate for disappointment, it also has the power to erase the real suffering of the woman the artist depicts. There is a selfishness in the artist's work that makes the woman in it hard to see."

Theme/Paragraph One: The poem suggests that, by depicting the woman's face time after time, the artist is paradoxically imitating (and re-imitating) something that is inimitable and singular. This hints at a sinister side to the artist's efforts to bring his 'dream' to canvas.

- The poem begins with the word 'One', making the singularity of the artist's fantastic vision the starting point of the poem. Rossetti draws our attention forcefully to the woman's face and its uniqueness, but it is a uniqueness that the painter constantly reiterates in each new painting. The repetition is then emphasized by the repetition of 'One' at the beginning of the second line. It is as if there is something impossible about this repetition, as the unique thing paradoxically happens twice; it is as if the singleness of the woman is itself a kind of fantasy. [*AO1 for making an interpretative point, and for quoting judiciously, AO2 for close analysis of language.*]
- The fantastical repetition is echoed by the poem's form. 'In an Artist's Studio' is a Petrarchan sonnet, so the same two rhyme sounds, 'ess' and 'eans/eens', repeat for the first eight lines of the poem. This repetition creates the same effect the poem describes, of the same face reappearing, slightly changed in different places. [*AO2, but notice that the point is not simply that the poem has repeated sounds, but that these support the meaning of the poem.*]
- We begin to get the sense that, behind the various guises, the sameness of the face is not simply

consistency. It is something more unsettling. The poet wants us to feel penned in by the image. Though the artist's model 'sits or walks or leans', these varying poses do not change the fact that the woman is imprisoned in the paintings. [*AO1 here is met by my interpretative point that there is something unsettling about the depiction of the woman, AO2 for pointing out that this is achieved by the play of difference and repetition.*]

Theme/Paragraph Two: As the poem proceeds, Rossetti emphasises how the artist's fantasy, as it takes form in his work, conceals reality, and threatens to efface the woman's identity.

- First, the figure is 'hidden behind screens', and then we see her in a variety of costumes. A Queen, a saint, and crucially, a 'nameless girl'. This namelessness suggests that even though the paintings are all of the same woman, she loses her selfhood in these paintings, and becomes merely a model for the fantasy that the painter has. [*Even though this is an interpretative point and therefore scores against AO1, we are talking about language by considering the possible meanings of nameless.*]
- When the poet writes, 'A saint, an angel — every canvas means / The same one meaning, neither more or less', the sameness of the meaning cancels out the difference between saint and angel. The line is split by a dash into two equal segments, which mark a **caesura** (*a kind of pause*) so that the different costumes are all balanced against the true

'meaning' of the painting. Every canvas, 'means/ the same one meaning'.[2] Rossetti here **enjambs** the line, so that the meaning of the woman's face seems important, but that meaning is snatched away by the next line, creating suspense, and a sense that the "meaning" is hidden, in the same way that the woman herself is hidden by the painting.[3] [*In this section I have really gone for the AO2 points, but note that I am not just pointing out that there is a caesura, or that there is enjambment. I am saying that these features create an effect that mirrors the theme.*]

Theme/Paragraph Three: Ultimately, the meaning of the paintings is nothing to do with the woman, but is entirely the dream of the artist. It is his fantasy she represents.

- Rossetti tells us that the painter 'feeds upon her face by day and night', implying that there is something almost vampiric about the artist's need for the woman he paints. The difference of night and day is cancelled out, like the other differences in the poem, so that both situations are the same to him. From this, we can infer that the sameness is a result of his need. [*AO1 here for interpreting the artist's need for the woman. Note that Rossetti* implies *and we* infer. *The writer always implies, and the reader always infers.*]
- The poem shows us that the artist wants the woman to be 'true' and 'kind', unlike the disappointments that we assume have arisen from his relationship with the real woman. However, Rossetti also shows us that the

real woman whom the artist has drawn has experienced 'sorrow', so the painter himself may have caused the disappointments. [*AO1, this is another interpretative point.*]

- The repetition of 'not as she is', in the final two lines, works in the same way as the repetition of 'one' at the beginning of the poem, but now we see the transformation of the face into the 'dream' of the artist. It is not simply that the artist is disappointed with the real woman; there is something sinister about this, about his need to replace the real world with a dream one. [*Here we pick up points for AO2, by talking about how Rossetti uses the pattern.*]

Conclusion

For my conclusion, I want to end with a slight twist. I'm going to summarise my point, but I want to widen the scope of my argument to make it more impactful. I'm therefore going to talk about gender in the poem, which has been bubbling under the surface of my answer.

> "'In an Artist's Studio' shows not only the way that an artist's fantasy might impose itself upon life, but the way that that fantasy might also reflect the power imbalance between men and women. The artist does not see the woman as she is, but as he dreams her, much as men have often seen women throughout history. Rossetti, by showing the dangerous nature of that fantasy, offers a way for the woman in the painting to speak back to the artist who has tried to dream her out of existence."

[*Remember there are no AO3 marks for context, nor AO4 marks for grammar and spelling, but that doesn't mean you don't want to talk about society or to spell words correctly. By pointing to a wider issue, I have a way of showing that I have thought quite hard about what the poem is doing. I am also still interpreting the poem in an 'exploratory' fashion, which is key to the top band of AO1.*]

COMPARATIVE MINI ESSAY

DANTE GABRIEL ROSSETTI'S 'THE PORTRAIT'

The Portrait
Dante Gabriel Rossetti

O Lord of all compassionate control,
O Love! let this my lady's picture glow
Under my hand to praise her name, and show
Even of her inner self the perfect whole:
That he who seeks her beauty's furthest goal,
Beyond the light that the sweet glances throw
And refluent wave of the sweet smile, may know
The very sky and sea-line of her soul.
Lo! it is done. Above the long lithe throat
The mouth's mould testifies of voice and kiss
The shadowed eyes remember and foresee.
Her face is made her shrine. Let all men note
That in all years (O Love, thy gift is this!)
They that would look on her must come to me.

*refluent -flowing (often flowing back as the tide does when it ebbs)

*lithe – thin and graceful
*mould – shape

Q2. In both 'In an Artist's Studio' and 'The Portrait', the poems' speakers describe attitudes towards the artist's work. What are the similarities and differences between the way the poems present these attitudes?

[8 marks]

Before we dive in...

The key thing to note here is the phrase 'the way the poems present these attitudes'. It is not so much the attitude that matters as what the poets do to present it. This puts us in AO2 territory.

The second poem is by the brother of the author of the first poem, Dante Gabriel Rossetti. Dante Gabriel is often thought to be 'the artist' in Christina's poem, so let's see how he talks differently about this portrait of a woman. In a way, this pairing really does show us the same idea presented differently. Both poems are also Petrarchan sonnets, (14 lines, of which the first six rhyme *abbaabba*) so we'll have to work hard to show the differences between the two poems.

This answer is only worth eight marks, so we want to point to keep the answer shorter. Mine is longer than you will be able to manage in the time, but it gives a sense of how to go about it. I think it is best to organise it around one key difference, and then make two or three points beneath that heading. Think of it like a larger version of one of the paragraphs in the previous answer. I will explain how and where we are hitting the marks.

I will structure the essay with two paragraphs and an introduction and mini-conclusion, but this is a shorter piece so don't worry as much about the number of paragraphs beyond the introduction and conclusion. If you have time for two, great! One paragraph will also work.

Mini Introduction

As you can see, this introduction really just sets the tone. I discuss the difference between the two poems' attitudes towards the art. Now in what remains we need to say how this is achieved by language, structure and form. We need to say how these attitudes are presented.

> "Both poets present the work of the artist as possessing a power over the person it depicts. In 'In an Artist's studio' the power of the work of art distorts the person, while in 'The Portrait', the work of art reveals the truth about the subject that only the artist has previously seen. In both poems, it is the artist's perspective that comes to matter by the end of the poem, but in 'In an Artist's Studio', this is portrayed from a distance, while in 'The Portrait, we are made to identify with the artist's perspective."

Mini Paragraph One

Here, I have made use of subject terminology ('sonnet', 'rhetorical', 'repetition', 'line'), and I have attached these to my claim about the difference of the two, in a way that meets the 'exploratory' and 'judicious' standards for the top band of AO2.

- Even though both poems are formally very similar, being sonnets, and even opening with the same rhetorical gesture of repeating the first word of the first line, they achieve different effects through similar techniques. The 'O' which Dante Gabriel begins his poem with is an address to Love, so that the repetition is an amplification of the passion that the speaker claims to possess. He is not dispassionately observing someone else's passion, but emphasising his own.
- While in Christina's poem, the woman depicted is 'hidden behind screens', Dante Gabriel uses the image of shining a light from his hand to make the picture 'glow', rhyming this word with 'show', to demonstrate that art reveals the truth. This ability to reveal or emphasise the truth is 'love's gift'. In Christina's poem, the woman is displayed in multiple costumes, but in Dante Gabriel's poem, it is natural imagery that unifies the different appearances. He speaks of 'the very sky and sealine of her soul'. He is making her into a landscape, and the sibilance here makes the line seem unified, repeating the S sound, the way different waves repeat the same shape. Landscapes are a single person's point of view, so in a way, what the speaker is saying is that his own view of the woman shows her as she really is, and brings her together into a single truth.

Mini Paragraph Two

Even though I am interpreting the poems' meanings, I have extended the discussion of language, structure and form, which is the key to AO2.

- [*here we pivot to our most important comparison.*] This unity is similar to Christina's view of the 'one face', but he means it as a positive. His own passion uncovers the beauty of nature. Dante Gabriel Rossetti's glow of passion is a stark contrast, then, to the 'dim' kind of light that we see in Christina Rossetti's poem, where the 'dream' makes everything the same. Indeed, even though 'dream' and 'dim' do not rhyme properly, she makes them rhyme at the end of her poem, to echo the distorting power of that dream. Unlike Dante Gabriel, who is intent on displaying the beauty of his painting to 'men', Christina wants us to see the falseness of the unity she displays, emphasising the contrasts between night and light in her poem.

Mini Conclusion

Again, here I have ended by pointing out the differences in attitude, and summarised the approach to presenting that attitude, in order to ensure that the examiner thinks I have met AO2.

> "For Christina Rossetti, men's passion expressed in art becomes oppressive, so she tries to emphasise passion's contradictions. Using the same pattern that Dante Gabriel Rossetti uses to bring different ideas together in the perspective of the artist, Christina Rossetti pries them apart."

A painting by Dante Gabriel Rossetti, featuring his muse Lizzie Siddal, whose face is sometimes thought to be the one mentioned in Christina Rossetti's poem

PAPER TWO: POEMS ON ROMANTIC PROPOSITIONS

ESSAY PLAN: KATHERINE PHILIPS'S 'AN ANSWER TO ANOTHER PERSUADING A LADY TO MARRIAGE'

An Answer to Another Persuading a Lady to Marriage
Katherine Philips

Forbear, bold youth, all's Heaven here,
And what you do aver,
To others, courtship may appear,
'Tis sacrilege to her.

She is a public deity,
And were't not very odd
She should depose her self to be
A petty household god?

First make the sun in private shine,
And bid the world adieu,
That so he may his beams confine
In complement to you.

But if of that you do despair,
Think how you did amiss,
To strive to fix her beams which are
More bright and large than this.

* aver – state or profess as fact.
* courtship – pursuing someone romantically, asking them to go out with you.
* sacrilege – an act that goes against religious law or teaching. Blasphemy.
* household god – a small statue of a god that watches over a family in their house.
* adieu – "goodbye" in French.

Q1. In 'An Answer to Another', how does the poet present the woman the "bold youth" is trying to persuade?

[24 Marks]

Introduction

As in plan one, I'm going to start by offering a summary. How does the poet present the woman? That means I need to say what I think the woman is like, and how the poet has made me think that.

> "In 'An Answer to Another', Katherine Philips presents the woman as entirely out of the bold youth's league. We see that she rejects his entreaties, or treats them as if they were beneath contempt, by using the exaggerated language of romance against itself. Many

men have claimed that a woman is a goddess, but if that were so, would they not consider it slightly inappropriate to try to date them? By making such a problem literal, Katherine Philips subtly attacks the fantasies and expectations of men."

Theme/Paragraph One: Philips positions the woman at an extraordinary distance from the youth. The poem is addressed to the youth but is not in the voice of the woman. It is as if she does not condescend even to talk to him.

- The distance of the speaker is most clearly emphasised by the speaker's insistence on changing the words of the youth. She translates what the youth is doing from 'courtship' to 'sacrilege'. This is a comic change, which fits with the use of other religious imagery, from 'heaven' to 'public deity'. As a goddess, the woman possesses the power to redefine words. The fact that the rhyme of the first stanza is on the words 'to her' stresses her importance. Hers is the perspective that matters, and she owns the language. [AO2 *here I am discussing the language and how it is used to create meaning. This would also score points for AO1, because from this language I am inferring something about the poem itself.*]
- For this reason, the youth is referred to as "bold" at the beginning. While some might think that being bold is a good quality, we see from his being told to "forbear", that he is too bold. He has dared to pursue

the woman. The speaker's statement seems like an exaggeration, and it sets a tone of comic exaggeration that helps us to see some of the problems with the language of love. [AO1, *this is a point about interpretation, backed up by judicious use of quotation.*]

- The problems can be seen most clearly when the lady is compared to the sun, which is totally indifferent to small things such as humans. The extended metaphor or conceit, here, where the speaker discusses the impossibility of making the sun shine in private, makes humorous the difficulty of thinking of the sun as human. The sun is personified as someone who speaks French, bidding the world adieu, but this exaggeration helps to remind the reader that this is in fact not true. The sun cannot do this because the sun is not human. [*AO1 and AO2: the AO1 element is made clear by translating the meaning of the conceit into my own terms, but I am also explaining that this works as a conceit, which is a particular use of language, so it hits AO2.*]

Theme/Paragraph Two: The power that Philips's speaker gives the lady comes from her beauty. It is this that allows her to be distant.

- The things that the woman is compared to include the sun and the skies, and it is their brightness that seem to matter. We are not told anything about the lady's personality. We are simply told of her glory. [*AO1. I have not quoted or analysed the language here, but it is a useful way of setting up my argument. It's fine to make a general point, just make sure that in every paragraph you have a quotation.*]

- When the speaker says 'all's heaven here', the phrase seems almost to divide the woman into pieces. Rather than saying all heaven's here, as in all of heaven is gathered in this one woman, we are told that all is heaven. This could mean something more like each individual part of the woman being described is heavenly. While this is flattering, and something common to love poetry as it describes women, again the attention is placed on features and not on personality. [*Philips is engaging with the tradition, common in poetry after the* ***Renaissance****, of what is called the* ***Blazon****.*[1] *It doesn't matter if you don't know the name of a term, though, just try to talk about what the language is doing and that will be enough for AO2.*]
- Indeed, the woman's personality, if we can tell anything from her refusal, seems haughty. If she has been kind to the youth at a previous point, the speaker does not think she is about to be kind to him now. [*AO1. Again, I have not quoted, but I have given a general interpretative point. Your answers will be shorter than mine, and quite a useful way of structuring the paragraph might be to think AO1 interpretative point (explain what a quotation means), AO2 (analyse the effect in detail), and then back to AO1, a more general summary.*]

Theme/Paragraph Three: As she makes the goddess powerful by placing her outside of humanity, however, Philips also points out the

potential for this kind of language to dehumanise women.

- The speaker says that the woman would not 'depose herself to be/ a petty household god', and what she implies by saying that is that the woman would not be treated as an equal, if she became a wife. Instead she would be like a household god. These are statues of gods that only matter within the house; they are objects and not humans, and while in theory they are worshipped, they are also trapped inside. A human is more important. [*AO1 for interpretation. This would be a high-scoring point for AO1, because I am thinking about the implications of the events of the poem. Think of it like this: If I analyse some lines from John Keats, such as 'now more than ever seems it rich to die/ to cease upon the midnight with no pain', and say this means Keats wants to die without feeling any pain, I am making an AO1 point. If I say that the word 'cease' helps to reinforce that because it is a gentle sounding word, unlike, say, croak, that's AO2.*]
- We get the sense that the youth wants control over the woman when the speaker uses the analogy of the sun shining 'in complement to you'. In complement to you seems to imply that the woman should serve the man. [*AO1 for interpretation justified by a quotation.*]
- As the speaker says, providing this service would require the lady to 'depose' herself. To depose means to remove from power, so it is clear that what matters here is the power balance between men and women. The word has connotations of violence, war or treachery, so it makes the romantic relationship discussed in the poem seem to have more to do with

politics and power than we would expect. Likewise, the word 'confine' also reminds us that limits are being set, and that what is at stake is control. [*AO2. One of the key things you can do for AO2 is to talk about the connotations of a word, the associations that a word brings with it from the ways it is normally used. If I 'execute a backflip' it seems to me that the word has a kind of military connotation, and is related to 'execute' as in to kill. It is possible to prosecute a relationship as one prosecutes (as in carries out) a military campaign, but if I say it like that, it's clear that I mean something different from 'having' a relationship.*]

Conclusion

For the conclusion I want to end simply with a summary of what I have been arguing, but I also want to make a final point if I can. Here, by analysing a moment from the very end of the poem, I can score a final couple of points. I choose the discussion of the 'beams', which are the woman's eye beams. I can also use this metaphor in my own words to make my conclusion seem like I have wrapped the whole poem up.

> "The woman is presented as taking advantage of the possibilities of language used by men in order to reclaim some power from them. The last lines of the poem refer to the woman's beams, which refer to the rays of light the youth claims come from her eyes, but they might also suggest that she sees clearly. If that is the case, then she sees through the inflated rhetoric of the youth who pursues her, and knows that it is hollow

in a world where women are not treated as equals. They are given power in poetry, and the lady has no desire to come down from the pedestal a poet would place her on to be treated badly as a wife. In refusing, she also criticises a society that claims to worship women but which denies them full participation and equality."

A Roman household deity from the first or second century AD.

COMPARATIVE MINI ESSAY

ELIZABETH BARRET BROWNING'S 'LORD WALTER'S WIFE'

From 'Lord Walter's Wife'
Elizabeth Barrett Browning

"But why do you go?" said the lady, while both sate
under the yew,
And her eyes were alive in their depth, as the kraken
beneath the sea-blue.

"Because I fear you," he answered;—"because you are
far too fair,
And able to strangle my soul in a mesh of your gold-
colored hair."

"Oh, that," she said, "is no reason! Such knots are
quickly undone,
And too much beauty, I reckon, is nothing but too
much sun."

"Yet farewell so," he answered;—"the sunstroke 's fatal
at times.

I value your husband, Lord Walter, whose gallop rings
still from the limes."

"O, that," she said, "is no reason. You smell a rose
through a fence:
If two should smell it, what matter? who grumbles, and
where's the pretence?"

* sate – an obsolete form of "sat".
* kraken – a fabled giant squid.

Q2. In both 'Lord Walter's Wife' and 'An Answer to Another', the poets explore the language of love between men and women. What are the similarities and differences in the way the poets present this subject?

[8 marks]

Before we dive in...

Again, in this question, I think it's best to stick to one key difference, and either have one other similarity or difference. In this essay, I start by describing the two poems, and what I think they're about, and then move on to explaining it. Here, I start with the second poem, just because we have already written about the first one. I then make some small comparisons as I go along, before pivoting to the key comparison. Remember, my version of this is longer than what you'll manage in your exam. That's just so I can also show you more ways of looking at the poem.

Mini Introduction

Here, I offer my summary of what the two poems share in terms of subject and perspective.

> "In both poems, the poets present the language of romance as something unrealistic. In particular, the way that men talk about love reinforces unrealistic ideas about women that constrain them in their lives. While 'An Answer to a Youth' presents a woman rejecting a man, and 'Lord Walter's Wife' presents a woman apparently pursuing him, both poems use these stories to undermine men's expectations of women."

Mini Paragraph One

Here I talk about how the second poem uses language to create its perspective, and briefly compare it to the first poem.

- Rather than be self-sacrificing or modest, the women featured in these two poems speak out against these ideals. In 'Lord Walter's wife', the most important method that Barrett Browning uses to present her criticism of the way men talk about women is the deliberate undermining of the metaphors that the male speaker uses. He claims that the beauty of Lord Walter's wife means that she is able to 'strangle my soul in a mesh of your gold coloured hair'. While this is already slightly ridiculous, and the sibilance [*the repetition of* S *sounds*] of 'strangle my soul in a mesh' adds to the sense that the man is exaggerating, the main point the woman makes in reply is that this is simply impossible. 'Such knots are quickly undone', she says, and this might serve as a metaphor for all of the man's attempts to pin the woman down in the language of romance. She undoes the knots that he weaves, and points out that the language is not accurate.

- The speaker is deliberately down to earth, saying that 'too much beauty, I reckon, is nothing but too much sun'. Even in the first couplet there is something slightly ridiculous in the description of her eyes as 'alive in their depth like the kraken beneath the sea-blue'. While eyes that are blue as the sea sound romantic, eyes with a giant squid inside them do not. The comic effect is similar to the lines in 'An Answer' where the sun is made to 'bid the world adieu'. In both poems the exaggeration is taken to an extreme that undermines the language that men use.

Mini Paragraph Two

Here I discuss the key difference in terms of how the poems present their subject. For me, this is the way the second poem works as a dialogue, which I discuss in detail.

- The key difference between the two poems is Barrett Browning's presentation of the poem as dialogue. Philips takes advantage of the one-sidedness of the answer. She does not even allow the youth's own terms, such as 'courtship', to be used and insists on it being 'sacrilege'. Perhaps the clearest view of the difference can be seen in the way that Philips's image of the sun differs from Browning's image of the rose. Lord Walter's wife, according to the metaphor, has no need to be faithful because more than one man can smell a rose, and Philips's lady cannot be kept inside, because the sun cannot either. Both point to the way that the image does not fit the woman. A woman is not really like a rose or like the sun. However, in Barrett Browning's poem this undermining comes as part of a demand that the man acknowledges Lord Walter's wife as an equal. Philips's poem would not 'depose' itself like that. It could be that the woman needs what little power she has.

- The couplet structure of 'Lord Walter's Wife' helps to reinforce the sense of it as a dialogue, rather than a one-sided expression by the man. While the man offers reasons to refuse her, Browning suggests that these are not really related to the woman as a person, they are either to do with a fear of women, or a loyalty of men to 'Sir Walter'.

Mini Conclusion

Finally, I try to make a brief general point, which sums up the difference between the poems.

> "Both poets want a real conversation to occur between men and women. Browning, however, presents a woman trying to achieve that, to move past what she calls 'the pretence', while Philips takes more joy in making fun of the hypocrisy of men."

BROWNING'S WIFE, ELIZABETH BARRETT

Elizabeth Barrett was a poet in her own right before her marriage with Robert Browning with whom she eloped, against her father's wishes, to Italy. Her "Sonnets from the Portuguese" hold a high place in English literature; "Aurora Leigh" is a novel in poetic form which won immediate success on its publication in 1857.

A portrait of Elizabeth Barrett Browning.

PAPER THREE: POEMS ON MEMORIES

ESSAY PLAN: EDWARD THOMAS'S 'ADLESTROP'

Adlestrop
Edward Thomas

Yes. I remember Adlestrop—
The name, because one afternoon
Of heat the express-train drew up there
Unwontedly. It was late June.

The steam hissed. Someone cleared his throat.
No one left and no one came
On the bare platform. What I saw
Was Adlestrop—only the name

And willows, willow-herb, and grass,
And meadowsweet, and haycocks dry,
No whit less still and lonely fair
Than the high cloudlets in the sky.

And for that minute a blackbird sang
Close by, and round him, mistier,

Farther and farther, all the birds
Of Oxfordshire and Gloucestershire.

* unwontedly – unexpectedly, in a manner not previously done.
* meadowsweer – a kind of grass.
* haycock – a pile of cut hay heaped in a field.

Q1. How does the poet present the speaker's experience of Adlestrop?

[24 marks]

Introduction

Once again, the question is how does the poet **present** the **speaker's experience**? We can break this down into two key points. We need to be able to describe this 'experience' — what we think it is — and offer an explanation of why we think that is. In the introduction we can't list all of the techniques the poet uses to present the experience, but we can say what he presents it as. A quotation is always helpful, to show that we're starting strong.

> "In 'Adlestrop', Edward Thomas presents the speaker's experience of a train journey that sticks in the mind because of its departure from routine. 'Adlestrop/ the name' comes to stand in for a moment of surprising beauty, and of stillness in a busy world, that the speaker returns to, but which seems slightly beyond his grasp."

Theme/Paragraph One: At first, Adlestrop seems to be not so much a place as a time. The poem introduces it as a memory.

- The speaker tells us 'I remember Adlestrop', but we are not told about the place. Rather we are told what happened to the speaker when he saw the name 'Adlestrop'. [*AO1, this is a general summary of the point. I have paraphrased the poem following the quotation. This proves that I have understood it up to a point.*]
- The importance of time is reinforced by Thomas, as the first stanza makes two of its rhymes on words that both have to do with time. 'Afternoon' and 'June', each ending the line, clearly position the speaker within a specific moment. [*AO2 because I am analysing the way the form helps the meaning. Rhyme words are often important, both because a reader might pause on them as the line breaks, and because the repeated sound makes them stick slightly more in the mind.*]
- At the same time, however, the moment represented by Adlestrop is unexpected. It is not simply part of the progress of time, like the ticking of a clock. Thomas hints that the intensity of the speaker's experience of Adlestrop stems from a slightly mismatched sense of time. In the third line, for example, there are too many syllables for the **iambic tetrameter** rhythm: 'the express train' contains too many unstressed syllables, and it is almost as if the speeding train is trying to cram too much in.[1] This cramming is what Adlestrop interrupts when the train stops 'unwontedly'. [*AO2, again I'm talking about form. It is unlikely that you'll need to talk about metrical stress in your exam, but see*

the endnote if you are interested. What you do always want to think about, however, is how the poet is controlling the experience of time. Are the lines long or short? Are lots of sounds repeated? Read the poem aloud and see how fast the lines feel to you.]

- That surprise might explain the jerkiness of some of the lines. The use of the caesuras in the last line of the first stanza and the first line of the second, for example, create stops within individual lines, breaking them into smaller units, so Thomas gives the reader the experience of their usual sense of time being interrupted. [*AO2, again, I'm talking about language and form as a way of changing the experience of the poem. See the endnote iii on caesuras.*]

Theme/Paragraph Two: If Adlestrop is outside the regular time of the express train, it also seems to be outside of the progress of history.

- The express train is modern and urban, whereas Adlestrop seems to be a very rural place. As Thomas says, 'no one went and no one came', because the train does not normally stop there. The station thus offers a contrast to the poet's normal, presumably urban, experience. [*AO1, for talking about meaning, backed up with a quotation.*]
- The use of the word 'bare' is interesting here. I would expect bare to be used about trees, rather than a building like a platform. By using this word, Thomas seems to suggest that the speaker is experiencing not simply an empty platform, but a more natural world. [*AO2, for talking about the* ***connotations*** *of a word.*[2]]

- You might expect the word stop, which rhymes with Adlestrop, to feature somewhere. It does not, but, when the train 'drew up' Thomas uses a similar sound. Adlestrop is where time almost – but does not quite – stop as the train goes on. [*AO2 for talking about language, structure and form. Even if a word isn't there, if we expect to hear it, it can inform our reading. If I say 'I place no one above you, my dove', I bet your mind will link this with the word love.*]

Theme/Paragraph Three: Even though 'Adlestrop' is experienced as 'a moment', it becomes a place as the speaker comes to recognise it.

- While the first two stanzas of the poem are stop-start, with sentences ending in the middle of a line, the next two stanzas are whole sentences. Thomas even uses enjambment between the second and third stanzas, as if Adlestrop is suddenly opening up. We are told that he sees only the name, but that is not the end of the sentence, when the next stanza begins, there is an 'and' that introduces the world around the train station. [*See note ii for a discussion enjambment. This is talking about language, structure and form, so AO2.*]
- The speaker now looks past the name Adlestrop, and he sees a variety of natural things, like herbs and trees and hay. If the platform was bare like a dead tree, then suddenly he sees the living world. At this moment, as well, the language becomes more old-fashioned. The speaker describes the plants as 'not a whit less still and lonely fair', which seems like an archaic register [*The poem is from 1914, and even then, you would be unlikely to describe something as 'lonely fair'.*]. It is as

if the place of nature has connected him to an ancient history. [*AO2 for talking about language form and structure, AO1 for talking about the comparison between the different kinds of objects visible in the poem.*]

- It is because he is now connected to the natural world that the blackbird sings, and it seems that the speaker is finally listening. The birds sing 'farther and farther', which does not mean that their voices are getting louder. Instead, it means that the speaker is tuning in to the world around him, which is Adlestrop. [*AO1. My inferring that the speaker is 'finally' listening is not the only interpretation of the poem. It is plausible, however, because birds would likely be singing the whole time, but the speaker would remember one as the first, and this is the moment he really connects to the place and to the moment.*]

Conclusion

For the conclusion, I am offering a small summary of what I think the poem tells us not only about the speaker's experience, but about life in general. This is what I think the poet wants us to learn from it.

> "In 'Adlestrop', Edward Thomas shows us how an experience can open out into a wider one when we least expect it, and how a memory can be particularly resonant in a way that counteracts the effects of modern life. Though this is only a 'moment', and indeed perhaps appeals only because it is one moment, it contains more life than the speaker's usual

experience and so lives on the memory. The poem seems to suggest that we should get in touch with the natural world, and that doing this will create memories that last far longer than the business-like experiences we normally waste our time with."

The Adlestrop railway sign was relocated to a bus stop when the railway station closed in the 1960s. Copyright © Judy Dean.

COMPARATIVE MINI ESSAY
THOMAS HARDY'S 'THE SELF UNSEEING'

The Self Unseeing
Thomas Hardy

Here is the ancient floor,
Footworn and hollowed and thin,
Here was the former door
Where the dead feet walked in.

She sat here in her chair,
Smiling into the fire;
He who played stood there,
Bowing it higher and higher.

Childlike, I danced in a dream;
Blessings emblazoned that day;
Everything glowed with a gleam;
Yet we were looking away!

* emblazoned – decorated.

Q2. Both 'Adlestrop' and 'The Self Unseeing' feature speakers who discuss a particular memory of a place. What are the similarities or differences in the way the poems present those memories?

[8 marks]

Mini Introduction

Remember, we are looking for a key difference or similarity to structure our argument around: some way in which the language of the poem encodes an essential difference in attitude.

Here, I offer my summary of what the two poems share in terms of subject and perspective. I have also summarised how I think their perspectives differ.

> "In both 'The Self Unseeing' and 'Adlestrop', the speakers reminisce about a particular place from their past; but while Thomas tries to show a moment of stillness, a moment that he can recall paying attention to, Hardy shows the way that time can escape you, how the ordinary things that you value can slip away, without you noticing."

Mini Paragraph One

Here I talk about how the second poem uses language structure and form to create its perspective, and briefly compare it to the first poem. Even though I open by talking about 'Adlestrop', I talk more about Hardy.

- Thomas's 'Adlestrop' begins with its memory. It is a moment that has stuck with the speaker — as he asserts, 'Yes I remember' — but things are different in Hardy's poem. He remembers because he has returned to the site of his memory. Hardy's poem begins in the world of the present, showing the decay of time. The floor is described as 'ancient', as well as 'footworn and hollowed and thin'. The use of these three adjectives by themselves on a single line serves to emphasise the process of decay. Because the adjectives come after the word 'floor', it is as if we are watching time work on the floor, making it footworn and hollow and thin. Thomas's poem is situated entirely inside the memory, whereas Hardy draws attention to the way his two worlds interact. When the 'dead feet' walk into the poem, Hardy signals how much is lost.

Mini Paragraph Two

Here I discuss the key difference in terms of how the poems present their subject. For me, this is the way that Hardy describes not seeing things, whereas Thomas is remembering sights and sounds.

- One of the key ways that Hardy signals the loss of the world he remembered is through the use of words of position, such as 'here' and 'there'. As we read the poem, we cannot know where the 'here' is, or the 'there'. While we imagine Hardy taking us round the room, showing us the location, the lack of position the reader has in actual space mirrors the lack of position the speaker has in time.

- In 'Adlestrop' on the other hand, once the speaker's eyes move past the 'bare platform' there is an abundance of things worth describing. Thomas's rhythm becomes less regular even as the syntax becomes more complicated, as he sees the connections between things, whereas Hardy is trying to will himself into seeing. It is because of his attempt to recapture things he cannot see that Hardy talks about the music. The poem seems to bring echoes of the music to life in its metre, which becomes more regular in the final stanza beginning 'childlike I danced in a dream'. This is a moment when time stops – whereas, in Hardy's poem, time has already passed.

Mini Conclusion

Finally, I try to make a brief general point, which sums up the difference between the poems.

"Both poems end by lumping things together, remembering too many things to take in with a single glance. In 'Adlestrop' this is 'all the birds', while in 'The Self Unseeing' it is simply 'everything'. However, Hardy's poem points out that he could have seen these things, as the title suggests. By listening to the birds, the speaker of 'Adlestrop' is able to imagine what he might see. Hardy on the other hand has to settle for admitting that he was looking away. It is that sense of self-blame which really distinguishes the speaker's attitudes to their memories. Hardy conveys this regret by taking the place away from his speaker, while Thomas's poem keeps giving its speaker more and more to see and think about."

Thomas Hardy, looking appropriately dour.

PAPER FOUR: POEMS ON YEARNING

ESSAY PLAN: ANDREW MARVELL'S 'THE MOWER TO THE GLOW WORMS'

The Mower to the Glow Worms
Andrew Marvell

Ye living lamps, by whose dear light
The nightingale does sit so late,
And studying all the summer night,
Her matchless songs does meditate;

Ye country comets, that portend
No war nor prince's funeral,
Shining unto no higher end
Than to presage the grass's fall;

Ye glow-worms, whose officious flame
To wand'ring mowers shows the way,
That in the night have lost their aim,
And after foolish fires do stray;

Your courteous lights in vain you waste,
Since Juliana here is come,

For she my mind hath so displac'd
That I shall never find my home.

* mower – a gardener who cuts grass.
* portend – predict or promise, suggest that something is going to happen.
* presage – predict or foreshadow.
* officious – efficient or bossy or following the rules.
* matchless – without peer, extremely good.

Q1. How does the poet present the speaker's feelings about the glow worms?

[24 marks]

Introduction

This time it is the speaker's **feelings** that we are trying to decipher, and how the poet presents these. One way of thinking about this is by always asking yourself the questions 'what kind of person would be saying this?' 'What kind of situation would I say this in?'. In this way, reading a poem is a little bit like being a psychologist, analysing a patient. What do they really mean when they say their father was scary like a dinosaur? Perhaps they are really scared they might lose their father, that he might, like a dinosaur, go extinct. Perhaps not. But you get to the feelings by exploring the shades of meaning. Here, I introduce my argument by summarising both what happens in the poem, and the way this points to certain feelings that I think the Mower reveals as he talks about the glow worms.

"In 'The Mower to the Glow Worms', Andrew Marvell depicts a speaker who addresses the glow worms as if they were wasting their time. They shine in vain because the woman that the mower loves, 'Juliana', has confused him to the point that he does not notice their beauty—or so we might think at first. However, the Mower has talked about these glow worms at length for the whole poem, and it seems as if, rather than dismiss them as irrelevant to his love for Juliana, he has made them into a symbol for his love, and possibly for the rejection he has experienced from Juliana. He follows her as if he were chasing 'after foolish fires'."

Theme/Paragraph One: The glow worms are introduced affectionately, as the poet talks to them directly. He places the glow worms within a balanced natural world, one to which he normally belongs.

- By referring to their light as 'dear' he implies that he is acquainted with the light, it is a precious memory. As a mower, that makes sense: he is used to their light 'in the summer evening', and he then connects this light to the song of the nightingale. [*AO1 for offering an interpretation backed up by a quotation.*]
- The use of the word 'matchless' seems at once to refer to the beauty of the nightingale's song and the fact that the nightingale is lonely. When the mower later refers to the worms as 'shining to no higher end/ than to presage the grasses' fall', the reader likewise gets a

sense of loneliness or wistfulness. The light of the glow worms is wasted. [*AO2 for talking about the connotations of the words.*]

- Marvell uses a metaphor of comets, which were once thought to predict important events, but his 'country' versions of the comets do not do any such thing. We might even infer from these lines that the mower is talking about his own station: as a humble gardener, perhaps he feels embarrassed about his love for Julia, and he compares the light that the comets emit to the poem he is speaking. [*Note once again that we infer: the writer implies, the reader infers. When we infer, we tend to score AO1 points, but here by discussing the metaphor, we also score for AO2.*]

Theme/Paragraph Two: By reminding him of his social station, the glow worms then function as a guide for the confused mower.

- The use of the word 'officious', which means both effective and carrying out a duty, deepens the connection between himself and the worms. He is a mower, and his place is working in the garden, just as the duty of the glow worms is to guide him home. [*AO2, we are talking about the connotations of the words, though this should count towards AO1 too.*]
- The steady rhythm of the poem, its short rhyming lines of **iambic tetrameter**, reinforce the sense that the wandering is corrected by the glow worms. [*AO2, for talking about language structure and form. If we really wanted to push the argument here, we could argue that the shortened word wand'ring is corrected from the more normal use of the word*

'wandering', and so we could say that the poem stops the mower's wandering.]

- In the same way, nature itself is curiously ordered in the poem. The nightingale studies and meditates for her song, rather than simply singing it. By contrast, the fires of men are foolish, and the passion of the mower seems to be, like the fires, slightly against nature. The **alliteration** of 'foolish fires' hints at their artificiality, suggesting that perhaps the mower's love has confused him, causing him to defy the natural order.[1] [*AO1 and AO2. The more general point about the mower's love being against nature is AO1: I am describing what I think the content of the poem is, what it wants to say, but I get there partly by looking at how it says it, including talking about the alliteration, which covers AO2.*]

Theme/Paragraph Three: In spite of the way that the glow worms might seem to humble him and his love, the mower insists on his right to wander.

- The final stanza of the poem, which asserts that the mower shall never find his 'home', seems to show him not only intoxicated by the light he sees in Juliana, but also that this light has affected how he interprets everything he has seen. You might say that love has turned his world upside down. [*AO1 for interpretation backed up by a quotation.*]
- In this way, even though when the mower looks at nature he sees a variety of hopeless things, which remind him of the hopelessness of his love, by making that connection, he allows himself to think that love is natural. [*AO1 for interpretation backed up by a*

quotation. The word 'courteous', used to describe the lights, normally means 'polite', but here in the seventeenth century, it would also mean 'with the manners of the court'. As there's no AO3 marks and you can't be expected to know that, it won't matter for our essay plan, but think about this. There was once a tradition called courtly love, where a man would perform elaborate displays of affection for a woman. The court, being in town, was defined in opposition to the country. Here it seems as if perhaps the rules which 'courteous' might imply are being rejected by the mower. He loves Juliana too much to be guided by rules.]

Conclusion

For the conclusion I want to end with a summary of what I have been arguing, but I also want to make a final point if I can. This is not an AO2 point of analysis, but an AO1 point. While I have been talking about disorder in the poem — the way love confuses us — I think the poem isn't only about confusion. What would be the point in that? Instead, it guides us through confusion, so I try to explain how it does that.

"By using the glow worms as a mirror for his mind, the mower is able to order his thoughts, even though the order he is presenting is a disorder. In this poem Marvell shows a speaker who is capable of 'wand'ring' in his own thoughts and feelings. Perhaps he is saying that this is what love feels like: a confusion that nevertheless seems to make sense. Though the speaker will never find his home, that is what he wants, and the glow worms guide him in that. In a way he shows how love distorts our vision, changing everything it touches in a way that resembles the **pathetic fallacy**, but the poem also implies that by understanding that experience, one can wander in it."[2]

A glow worm at night.

COMPARATIVE MINI ESSAY

LORD TENNYSON'S 'THE PRINCESS'

from 'The Princess'
Alfred, Lord Tennyson

Now sleeps the crimson petal, now the white;
Nor waves the cypress in the palace walk;
Nor winks the gold fin in the porphyry font.
The firefly wakens; waken thou with me.

Now droops the milk-white peacock like a ghost,
And like a ghost she glimmers on to me.

Now lies the Earth all Danaë to the stars,
And all thy heart lies open unto me.

Now slides the silent meteor on, and leaves
A shining furrow, as thy thoughts in me.

Now folds the lily all her sweetness up,
And slips into the bosom of the lake.
So fold thyself, my dearest, thou, and slip

Into my bosom and be lost in me.

* cypress – a type of evergreen tree.
* porphyry – a kind of stone with crystals in it.
* font – fountain.
* Danae – a Greek goddess.

Q2. In both poems, the speakers describe natural scenes at night while talking about love. What similarities or differences are there in the ways the speakers present those scenes?

[8 marks]

Mini Introduction

Here, I offer my summary of what the two poems share in terms of subject and perspective. I have also summarised how I think their perspectives differ.

> "In both of these poems, Tennyson and Marvell use an image of the natural world at night-time to think about love. However, while Marvell uses a variety of different emblems to show how love intoxicates the mind, and makes nature respond to it, Tennyson uses the natural world as an image of love in order to strengthen the speaker's invitation to his lover."

Mini Paragraph One

Here I talk about how the second poem uses language to create its perspective, and briefly compare it to the first poem.

- Tennyson's poem begins with an image of the world reconciled in sleep. The crimson and the white petal, which in the daylight seem so different, are both blended into one another in the dark. Tennyson achieves this unity through his use of negatives and repetition (**anaphora**).[1] Everything is brought together by not doing anything, and also by being bound in the moment. What unites them is 'now', as the poet tries to tell his lover that 'now' is the moment that they should express their love. The sound of 'now' and 'nor' blend together, so that in its first **quatrain** the poem creates a still present.[2]
- The **assonance** of 'winks the gold fin in the porphyry front' both echoes that sameness and shows how difference is still suggestive.[3] Porphry is a kind of crystal and so its glitter suggests that the darkness is alive with the possibility of things coming together. Tennyson creates an undercurrent of liveliness. While in Marvell's poem, love makes the mower lonely, even in a 'matchless' song, here everything matches in the dark.

Mini Paragraph Two

Here I discuss the key difference in terms of how the poems present their subject. For me, this is the way that Tennyson tries to turn every action in his poem into a form of touching.

- Everything in Tennyson's poem is about contact, even a comet in the sky. Both poems contain an image of a comet, but Marvell's one is in the imagination while Tennyson's comes from the sky into the imagination. The glimmer of the peacock, likewise, glimmers 'onto' him, and the stars are like a Greek goddess who was famously impregnated by Zeus when he took the form of the stars. Every object in the poem becomes a metaphor for requited love. This transformation is quite similar to the one in Marvell, but the transformation is a way for the mower to order his own thoughts and to think about his love. In Tennyson, the love seems to be quite explicitly requited. The 'shining furrow' left by the comet blends both imagination and reality, showing the way one becomes the other, as the palapability of the speaker's desire transforms the natural world.

Mini Conclusion

Finally, I try to make a brief general point, which sums up the difference between the poems.

"In both poems, nature is the image of the speaker's love, and both poets are quite conscious of that, using nature's transformations as a metaphor for the way desire works on the speakers. It is not simply that the things they look at remind them of their love; their love makes them see things differently. The crucial difference is that Tennyson tries to make the play of transformation involve the lovers, while Marvell makes those transformations self-contained, 'shining to no higher end'."

PAPER FIVE: POEMS ON PERSEVERANCE

ESSAY PLAN: ARTHUR HUGH CLOUGH'S 'SAY NOT THE STRUGGLE NOUGHT AVAILETH'

Say Not the Struggle Nought Availeth
Arthur Hugh Clough

Say not the struggle nought availeth,
The labour and the wounds are vain,
The enemy faints not, nor faileth,
And as things have been they remain.

If hopes were dupes, fears may be liars;
It may be, in yon smoke concealed,
Your comrades chase e'en now the fliers,
And, but for you, possess the field.

For while the tired waves, vainly breaking
Seem here no painful inch to gain,
Far back through creeks and inlets making,
Comes silent, flooding in, the main.

And not by eastern windows only,
When daylight comes, comes in the light,

In front the sun climbs slow, how slowly,
But westward, look, the land is bright.

* Availeth – achieves.
* fliers – those who flee.
* main – the main tide.

Q1. In 'Say not the Struggle Naught Availeth', how does the poet present the speaker's feelings?

[24 marks]

Introduction

A slightly more general question this time. So we need to ask what the speaker's feelings are, and then we can proceed to explain how the poet presents these. While the poem's chief message might be relatively straightforward, the complexities of the speaker's feelings have to be unpacked bit by bit, so I'll keep the introduction brief.

> "In 'Say not the Struggle Naught Availeth', Arthur Hugh Clough presents the speaker attempting to console someone, perhaps himself, as he provides a series of analogies for the experience of adversity. Progress, he suggests, is invisible but still possible. The complexity of these analogies helps Clough to make the case that we need to look harder for signs of hope."

Theme/Paragraph One: Clough draws our attention to attention itself, and to how we look at things, from the very beginning of the poem.

- The poem opens with a statement of what should not be said. Aside from the first two words, the entire first stanza simply articulates the fear that whatever the struggle was, it has been in vain. There is something ironic about beginning a poem with the words 'say not', and proceeding to say precisely that thing. [*AO1 as I have made an interpretive point, and backed it up with a judicious quotation, even though it's a small bit of the text. I think this also counts as AO2, as we are really talking about how the* ***syntax*** *of the poem creates meaning.*[1]]
- Clough offers rhyme words that emphasise the desolate feelings, and the inability of things to change: 'faileth', which undermines 'availeth', and then 'vain', which points out that the problems 'remain'. [*AO2 for discussion of language structure and form.*]
- The rhythm, too, is slightly altered by the word 'say.' While every line of the poem is iambic tetrameter, the first word, 'say', is as pronounced in its stress as 'not', which creates a kind of lilting rhythm. [*AO2 for talking about form. Compare –it's* ***not*** *that* ***stru****ggle's* ***poin****tless* ***now,*** *with* ***Say not*** *the* ***stru****ggle* ***nought*** *av****ail****eth – can you hear the difference in rhythm based on where you place the emphasis? I would only advise talking about metre or stress it if you really think it makes a difference. Don't just force a point in, but here I think it works.*]
- The difference between what Clough is saying and what Clough does not want to say is tiny, but as the

poem develops we come to see that this might be the point. You might not notice the difference between success and failure, especially when the 'struggle' is still continuing, but that does not matter. [*AO1, this is an exploratory interpretation. What makes it exploratory, you ask? Well, think about it like this: I am translating what I think the meaning of the poem is into my own words, and I am slightly extending the point, trying to apply it to situations outside of the poem.*]

Theme/Paragraph Two: Clough therefore suggests that you might not be able to tell how well things are going, and that that doubt is a good thing.

- It might seem that saying 'hopes were dupes' reiterates the disappointment of the speaker, but Clough's speaker manages to translate that into a better kind of uncertainty. If you did not know you were going to be disappointed, you might not know that you are going to be rewarded. In that way we can see that the speaker is trying to reason himself into optimism using a logical sounding formulation. [*I am paraphrasing the meaning here, initially. That is the basic point for AO1, but then we take it further by trying to describe not just what the speaker is saying, but why he might be saying it. That can often help you find the upper reaches of the mark scheme.*]
- Clough makes use of **consonance** [*the repetition of consonants*] to emphasise the possibility that things are not what they seem.[2] 'Hopes' and 'dupes' sound

similar, but are not the same. 'Fears' and 'liars' likewise end with the same consonants (rs), and Clough uses this repetition to support the speaker's point that things might be better than they appear. It could really be the case that what is 'concealed' is that the 'comrades' now possess the field. [*AO2, for discussing language structure and form.*]

- The extended metaphors of the sun and of the tides make it seem as if the success is something that will come, that it is natural. [*AO2 for discussing language, but also AO1, for suggesting that this metaphor helps make the point that success in natural.*]

Theme/Paragraph Three: Clough makes the poem slightly more complicated, however, because part of the point is that the speaker's perspective needs to change.

- When the speaker refers to the battle which is going well out of sight, he rather pointedly excludes 'you' from the group. It is 'but for you', as in 'all but you', but also it is hard to hear it without thinking that it might be 'if it was not for you'. There is a hint here that the struggle the speaker has is with his own mood. [*AO1 for an exploratory interpretation, as I am thinking about the various possibilities of what the speaker means.*]
- The question of perspective can be seen again in the way the speaker describes the waves. Waves cannot actually be 'tired', nor can they break 'vainly', because they do not actually have a purpose. It is the speaker who gives them this purpose, through personification, and he is projecting his own mood onto them. By

describing the waves, he is really only describing his own feelings of despair and exhaustion, even as he suggests that everything will be alright in the end. [*AO1 for interpretation backed up by quotation.*]

- The sense that there is a problem with the speaker's own perspective is emphasised in the final stanza too, when the poet uses repetition to create the experience of the sun rising 'slow, how slowly'. The line before, 'when daylight comes, comes in the light', also creates a sense of movement in small steps or increments, and we might think that this shows the speaker's own impatience, the way that time drags when you are waiting for something. As the saying goes, a watched pot never boils, and here the sun, likewise, does not rise because the speaker is looking the wrong way. [*AO2, by talking about repetition, I am talking about language, structure and form.*]

Conclusion

Again, I'm going to keep things brief this time, but I'm going to analyse one more point in the poem in order to use it to make my own final summary of what I think the poem is saying.

> "Part of the point might be that the struggle is not only to carry on, but to see things differently. The final command of the poem to 'look' is a command to turn the head. The speaker is looking east, where he expects to see the sun rise, but in the west the land is bright. Clough seems to suggest that hope requires making the effort to look for it."

COMPARATIVE MINI ESSAY

LORD BYRON'S 'CHILDE HAROLD'S PILGRIMAGE'

from 'Childe Harold's Pilgrimage'
George Gordon, Lord Byron

Yet, Freedom! yet thy banner, torn, but flying,
Streams like the thunder-storm *against* the wind;
Thy trumpet voice, though broken now and dying,
The loudest still the Tempest leaves behind;
Thy tree hath lost its blossoms, and the rind,
Chopped by the axe, looks rough and little worth,
But the sap lasts,—and still the seed we find
Sown deep, even in the bosom of the North;
So shall a better spring less bitter fruit bring forth.

Q2. In 'Say Not the Struggle Naught Availeth' and '*Childe Harold's Pilgrimage*', the speakers discuss the importance of perseverance. What are the similarities and the differences in the ways the poets present their attitudes?

[8 marks]

Mini Introduction

Here we have two quite similar poems, so we really need to probe into the differences, and one helpful one that Byron has pointed out for us is the very confusing statement that freedom's banner 'streams like the thunder-storm against the wind'. What could that possibly mean? How could a banner stream *against* (as opposed to with) the wind? Why too is the thunderstorm against the wind? Try to come up with your own answers before you have a look at the explanation I attempt.

Here, I offer my summary of what the two poems share in terms of subject and perspective. I have also summarised how I think their perspectives differ.

> "In both poems, the speakers attempt to come to terms with temporary setbacks, and to suggest that endurance will allow them to see their way to a better future. However, where Clough's poem uses its metaphors to imply that what is crucial is the attitude of the speaker, who needs to change the way he looks at things, Byron uses the analogy of the seasons to project the eventual victory further into the future. Freedom, like the spring, cannot be stopped."

Mini Paragraph One

Here I talk about how the second poem uses language to create its perspective, and briefly compare it to the first poem.

- In 'Childe Harold's Pilgrimage', the defeat is embodied in the image of freedom's banner 'torn'. Like Clough, Byron is conjuring up images of military defeat, using the flag **metonymically** to suggest the armies of freedom. Byron very pointedly italicises the word 'against' when he describes the action of the flag. Even though the flag would be limp without the wind, he sees it as against the wind. This is not simply because he has a poor understanding of the aerodynamics of flags. Rather, Byron wants to suggest that the natural force of the wind finds a natural counter force. That even though defeat is natural, that defeat creates a dramatic image. It is the wind that makes the flag fly, and oppression that ignites the struggle for freedom.
- I would contend that Byron is describing not just the sound of the 'thunder-storm', but the image of lightning, which might look like an extremely tattered flag. Clough also uses images of nature to justify his eventual success, such as the waves breaking or the sun rising, but he does not oppose these to other kinds of nature. Byron on the other hand makes a bigger deal of defeat. Here, the trumpet voice of freedom is 'dying'. Nevertheless, through assonance, the trumpet sound carries the thunder onwards. The rhymes too suggest continuity: after 'wind', he stops using the **short 'i' sound** and uses the long one, so that the words 'flying', 'dying', 'rind', 'behind', and 'find' all have the same sound in them, helping to create a sense of endurance.[1]

Mini Paragraph Two

Here I discuss the key difference in terms of how the poems present their subject. In this case it is about the confidence of the speaker, and the way that the seasons signal Byron's speaker's confidence.

- Clough seems to want us to pay attention to the difference between sounds, between 'hopes' and 'dupes' for example, but Byron wants us to continue to hear the same trumpet voice. Byron's poem does talk about how the tree 'looks rough and little worth', but whereas Clough's poem is about learning to see things differently, developing a new attitude, Byron is saying that inside the tree is the promise of Spring and of success. It is a small difference, but it is one that speaks of a slightly different attitude. Byron seems more confident in his own perception, in his knowledge both that freedom has lost, and that it will win in the end.

Mini Conclusion

Finally, I try to make a brief general point, which sums up the difference between the poems.

> "The key difference between the ways the two poets present their speakers' attitudes to defeat could actually be summed up by the first two words of each poem. Byron chooses 'Yet Freedom!, and his poem is about the push and pull of defeat, the way that freedom returns like the spring. Clough opens with 'say not', and what he wants to do is help us learn to speak differently about setbacks. Byron wants to remind us

that it will not always be Winter; Clough wants to help us make it through the night."

A portrait of a brooding Lord Byron.

PAPER SIX: POEMS ON BIRDS

ESSAY PLAN: D. H. LAWRENCE'S 'HUMMING BIRD'

Humming Bird
D. H. Lawrence

I can imagine, in some otherworld
Primeval-dumb, far back
In that most awful stillness, that gasped and hummed,
Humming-birds raced down the avenues.

Before anything had a soul,
While life was a heave of matter, half inanimate,
This little bit chipped off in brilliance
And went whizzing through the slow, vast, succulent
stems.

I believe there were no flowers then,
In the world where humming-birds flashed ahead of
creation
I believe he pierced the slow vegetable veins with his
long beak.

Probably he was big
As mosses, and little lizards, they say, were once big.
Probably he was a jabbing, terrifying monster.

We look at him through the wrong end of the telescope
of time,
Luckily for us.

* primeval – from the dawn of time.
* inanimate – not alive, or motionless.
* succulent – tender or juicy.

Q1. In 'Humming Bird', how does the poet present the speaker's feelings about the hummingbird?

Introduction

Here I have offered a summary of what I think is happening in the poem. Sometimes, you might want to try to sum up what the total effect of form or language is – for example, 'the poem mocks military precision with the over precise language that it uses', or perhaps 'the excessive passion is shown in the flowing language.' If you only have time to summarise the themes, however, that's also fine.

> "In 'Humming Bird', D. H. Lawrence presents the speaker as entranced by the hummingbird. The bird is not simply beautiful but is presented as alive with an intensity that challenges the speaker's sense of scale. The actual tininess of the bird is not what matters; it connects the poet to larger forces. By looking at the

hummingbird, the speaker comes to understand the limitations of his own perspective on the natural world and his own place in that world. The bird thus becomes an emblem for the power of the imagination, which connects the poet to the natural world by allowing him to think of things outside the limitations of his own perspective."

Theme/Paragraph One: The poem places a lot of emphasis on the speaker himself and his perception of the bird. It is made clear from the beginning that we are not simply presented with the bird neutrally, as if observing through a window.

- Instead, the first line is about the speaker's power to 'imagine' the bird in some 'otherworld'. This distance between reader and the thing observed is repeatedly pointed out by the speaker himself. He gets in the way. The speaker twice says 'I believe', and 'probably'. It is as if thinking about the hummingbird undermines the speaker's certainty that what he describes is real, or really out there in the world. [*AO1, when I write* ***it is as if****, I am making a translation of the poem into my own language which is an interpretative point, but I have reached that point by thinking about language and about the way the poet uses qualifying phrases, such as 'I believe', so this should count towards AO2, too.*]
- By making him imagine this other world, the bird allows him to question the stability of his own world, and of civilisation itself. In the poem, the

hummingbird is an image that he cannot see clearly through the 'telescope of time'. This metaphor suggests that time itself is a human construct. It is a particular way of perceiving things that is human, and may not reach the actual truth. [*AO1 for judicious quotation and for an interpretative point, AO2 because I am talking about metaphor.*]

- By saying that the truth of the hummingbird cannot be seen by us, the speaker seems to imply that there is a disconnection between modern life and the natural world. [*AO1 for exploratory interpretation—I am trying to take the meaning of the poem beyond what it says about what happens in the poem, to see if it contains any more general lessons.*]

Theme/Paragraph Two: In spite of this disconnection, however, the liveliness of the hummingbird is undeniable, and it transfers some of its energy to Lawrence's speaker.

- In the second stanza, the liveness of the bird is emphasised by the rhythmic contrast between its 'whizzing' and the 'slow vast succulent stems'. In this second quotation there are three stresses clumped together, which serve to give the trees being described a kind of heaviness. Against this heaviness, the whizzing of the hummingbird is ever more lively. [*AO2 for talking about language and form. For those who are more curious about stress, see endnote i.*]
- The phrase 'bit chipped off in brilliance' makes the rest of the world seem like stone, while this small piece chipped off shines. Lawrence uses this stone metaphor to describe the way the hummingbird's

flight looks like a small piece of rock being chipped off from a larger one, but the metaphor also serves another purpose. It is almost as if the poet is making a statue from the stone of the world, which as we have been told is 'half inanimate'. This piece is representative of the effort to make the statue. [*AO1 for exploratory interpretation, backed up by judicious quotation.*]

- The hummingbird, we are told, 'flashes ahead of creation'. Here Lawrence seems to be making use of two possible meanings of 'creation'. It could mean the world itself, but also the poetic impulse to make something. The bird is so fast that it is ahead of the whole world, but also ahead of the poet trying to write his poem. The poet cannot capture the vitality of the hummingbird, but he can create something from his attempt to do so. [*AO2 for talking about language. One of the most useful tricks a poet — or any writer — has is to play on the many meanings of a word. In a truly strong poem, every word carries extra shades of meaning. See the note on **Connotations**.*]

Theme/Paragraph Three: Making the bird the embodiment of life and of the creative imagination, Lawrence's speaker connects the hummingbird to ancient powers.

- It is perhaps for this reason that, early in the poem, we are told that the stillness of the primeval era also 'hummed'. This humming could suggest that the movement of the bird is like a distillation, or a concentration of the world before human understanding. Lawrence describes that world as alien and incomprehensible. [*AO1 for interpretation.*]

- The metaphor of the stillness 'gasping' and 'humming' therefore seems like a contradiction. It as is if the speaker cannot imagine what that stillness was really like, and so has to personify it, making it seem more human. At the same time as he does this, however, the hummingbird is made more strange. [*AO2 for discussing the language.*]
- The strangeness of the world that the hummingbird embodies is 'awful', and we are told that the 'big' hummingbird was a 'jabbing terrifying monster'. The speaker seems impressed with this awfulness, as if the present, when there are 'flowers', is somehow lesser. [*AO1 for judicious quotation. For the purpose of AO1 marks, it is often a good idea to embed quotations – that is to say, to make them part of a sentence, rather than simply say 'the poet says "XYZ". Writing 'it is at this moment that we truly see "the fury of aerial bombardment"' makes it clearer that you have digested what the sentence means than if you just say 'the poet discusses "the fury of aerial bombardment"'.*]
- There is something ironic in the casualness of the word 'big'. If you were trying to impress someone with the size and terrifying nature of an animal you would probably say huge, but that little word, 'big', repeated twice, again shows a kind of mismatch between the attempt to describe the true nature of the hummingbird, and the powers we have. In general, the poem points to the way the speaker finds his own language falling short. [*AO2 for discussing language.*]

Conclusion

For my conclusion, I want to return to a point I briefly touched on in my first paragraph that seems to me to be quite a good general way of ending things. This is because it broadens the focus of the poem from the hummingbird to the bigger issues of modern life and nature.

> "The speaker of 'Humming Bird' not only praises the bird, which gives him a vision of a past beyond words, but also uses it as a way of thinking about what seems like a modern decline. When the speaker concludes the whole poem with the casual phrase, 'luckily for us', he suggests that the hummingbird is almost too terrifying to be approached in its real condition. He implies, therefore, that we measure up poorly against the world that the real hummingbird comes from. Perhaps he is saying that civilisation, which has invented things like the telescope, has made us weaker. We are cut off from the true and seemingly violent world that the poet glimpses in the hummingbird's movements. The bird disturbs him, because it reminds him of a power that is beyond human understanding, which might mean we have to reject modern understanding to reclaim it."

A bust of D. H. Lawrence at Nottingham Castle. Copyright © Ozzy Delaney.

COMPARATIVE MINI ESSAY

PAUL LAURENCE DUNBAR'S 'SYMPATHY'

Sympathy

Paul Laurence Dunbar

I know what the caged bird feels, alas!
  When the sun is bright on the upland slopes;
When the wind stirs soft through the springing grass,
And the river flows like a stream of glass;
  When the first bird sings and the first bud opes,*
And the faint perfume from its chalice steals—
I know what the caged bird feels!

I know why the caged bird beats his wing
  Till its blood is red on the cruel bars;
For he must fly back to his perch and cling
When he fain would be on the bough a-swing;
  And a pain still throbs in the old, old scars
And they pulse again with a keener sting—
I know why he beats his wing!

I know why the caged bird sings, ah me,

When his wing is bruised and his bosom sore,—
When he beats his bars and he would be free;
It is not a carol of joy or glee,
But a prayer that he sends from his heart's deep core,
But a plea, that upward to Heaven he flings—
I know why the caged bird sings!

* opes — opens.

Q2. In both 'Humming Bird' and 'Sympathy' the speakers describe the feelings occasioned by observing a bird. What similarities or differences are there between the ways that the poets present these feelings?

[8 marks]

Before we dive in...

Aside from being about birds, these poems are actually fairly different. Not only because one is formal and one uses free verse, but because of their respective outlooks. When you're doing your unseen poetry exam, you won't know anything about the context, but Paul Laurence Dunbar was an African-American poet of the nineteenth century. Considering the oppression faced by Black Americans at that time, his claim that he knows why the caged bird sings has to take on the resonance of that oppression. Lawrence, on the other hand, was an Englishman from Nottinghamshire, who worked in the mid-twentieth century. This context would change their attitudes to nature, to the use of symbols, and to the idea of sympathy. But I only have the poems to go on, so I am going to try and show

how you can tease some of these ideas out without even mentioning the context.

Mini Introduction

Here, I offer my summary of what the two poems share in terms of subject and perspective. I have also summarised how I think their perspectives differ.

> "Both poets present the birds as symbols of the speaker's feelings. Rather than say they have feelings about the birds, it would be better to say that the birds help them to make sense of their feelings. However, in Paul Laurence Dunbar's poem 'Sympathy', the speaker claims to know the bird and to understand the source and depth of its own feelings, whereas in Lawrence's poem, the bird represents something unknowable. His poem could almost be said to be about the limits of sympathy."

Mini Paragraph One

Here I talk about how the second poem uses language to create its perspective, and briefly compare it to the first poem.

- In Dunbar, the bird and the speaker are bound together because they share their lack of freedom, while in Lawrence, the bird gestures to a hidden power that the poet wants access to. Unlike Lawrence's poem, Dunbar's is strictly metrical, and it rhymes in a set pattern. This helps to emphasise the fact that the bird is caged. The rhymes on the one hand could be said to be like the bars of the cage, but you could also see them as a way of reflecting the singing. If the poem suggests that the bird is not singing 'a carol of joy or glee', but rather 'a prayer that he sends from his heart's deep core', then it could be that the rhyme helps to reinforce the idea that poetry is a way of pushing back against oppression or control.

- In the first stanza, there is a slightly forced rhyme between 'slopes' and 'opes'. While this is just old-fashioned language, it also serves to disappoint our expectations that we might get the more obvious rhyme of 'hopes'. In this way, Dunbar seems to suggest that the caged bird is consoling herself for her disappointment, an action he strongly identifies with.

Mini Paragraph Two

Here I discuss the key difference in terms of how the poems present their subject. The key difference, I think, is that Dunbar wants to show that freedom and singing rise to counter restriction, and that through sympathy we can understand others, whereas Lawrence is more doubtful.

- On one hand, Lawrence does not identify with the bird, even though you sense he might want to. If he admires it for being a terrifying, jabbering monster, he also repeatedly says that he does not know things about it. Dunbar, on the other hand, is explicitly saying 'I know'. For Lawrence there is a world of nature that it is impossible to be truly in touch with. Dunbar arguably suggests something similar in the form of the cage – a device that functions to sever its captive from the natural world – but for Lawrence the key image is that of the telescope. Whereas, through the image of the cage, Dunbar stresses how social forces cut us off from nature, Lawrence's telescope stresses how the individual, despite their best effort to try to understand things, will continue to miss the point, and will thus find themselves at a remove from nature.

Mini Conclusion

Finally, I try to make a brief general point, which sums up the difference between the poems.

"In both, the bird seems to be presented as a symbol of the imagination, which is why he sings in Dunbar's poem and is associated with 'creation' in Lawrence's. However, Lawrence suggests that modern life puts us out of touch with imagination, while Dunbar implies that imagination persists even in the worst conditions."

A mural of Paul Laurence Dunbar in Washington D.C.

PAPER SEVEN: POEMS ON GRIEF

ESSAY PLAN: EMILY DICKINSON'S 'AFTER GREAT PAIN, A FORMAL FEELING COMES...'

'After great pain, a formal feeling comes...'
Emily Dickinson

After great pain, a formal feeling comes –
The Nerves sit ceremonious, like Tombs –
The stiff Heart questions 'was it He, that bore,'
And 'Yesterday, or Centuries before'?

The Feet, mechanical, go round –
A Wooden way
Of Ground, or Air, or Ought –
Regardless grown,
A Quartz contentment, like a stone –

This is the Hour of Lead –
Remembered, if outlived,
As Freezing persons, recollect the Snow –
First – Chill – then Stupor – then the letting go –

* ceremonious – as if at a ceremony, behaving solemnly.

* ought – aught/anything.
* regardless – heedless, without looks.
* quartz – a kind of crystal.

Q1. How does the poem present the speaker's experience of grief?

[24 marks]

Before we dive in...

We're going to try an extremely difficult one now. Emily Dickinson was a nineteenth century American poet who lived a very self-enclosed life, and wrote poems that often likewise seem enclosed, as if written in a private version of English. However, when you look at them closely, you see that what she is doing is pushing the words in ways that do make sense, but stretch our understanding of them. We can start with the word formal, here. What does it mean to feel formal?

Does Dickinson mean a feeling of formality, that we act more formally, more properly 'after great pain'? Or does it mean that the feeling itself is somehow 'formal', and does this have anything to do with the way that a poem is said to have a form? I think the answer to all of these is yes, and I'm going to try to show you how to write an answer to a question on a poem that may seem harder to understand.

Introduction

Once again, the introduction is going to offer a short summary of what we think the speaker's experience of grief is.

"In Emily Dickinson's 'After Great Pain', the speaker's experience of grief is presented as something that numbs her. Dickinson's poem seems to argue that the greatest power of grief is to weaken other feelings, to make them seem not like genuine feelings but simply the polite thing to do. The 'formal feeling' of the poem mirrors a mind's attempt to shut down the part of itself that is open to pain and to carry on functioning without it."

Theme/Paragraph One: Dickinson shows the effects of 'great pain' by removing any reference to a person experiencing the pain.

- Where one would expect an individual — an I, a you, or a he or she — who experiences the great pain, the pain and the feeling seem to take place in empty space. [*AO1, for interpretation. There is no quotation here, but that is because we are talking about an absence.*]
- Parts of the body are then personified, so we are told of the nerves 'sitting' and of the heart who 'questions'. However, even that question seems to be about the absence of a fixed and continuous identity. The heart is disorientated as to whom it is grieving for – the capitalised 'He' suggests it may be Jesus – or how long ago the death for which it is grieving took place. The poem thus blurs what may be a personal grief with the more universal suffering of the Christian messiah. It is as if the heart itself has lost track of both who people are and whether it is now or 'centuries before'. [*AO2*

for talking about personification. Note the way I have embedded the quotation at the end, which helps to show that I have been able to use the poem for my own purposes.]

- Dickinson describes the nerves as 'like Tombs', because tombs are a kind of ceremonial object, but her simile also brings with it the obvious association with death. If the pain the speaker has experienced is grief for the loss of a loved one, then the grief seems to have transferred the condition of death into the mind and body of the speaker. [*AO2 for talking about language, form and structure; but this analysis also supports speculation about the speaker's state of mind, which should give us points for AO1.*]

Theme/Paragraph Two: This deathliness, however, seems to be necessary to survival. Dickinson thus blurs the boundaries between life and death in both directions.

- Although Jesus 'bore' the great pain and died, he of course did so in order that he might live on and survive via resurrection. Likewise, the heart in the poem has to bear the pain of grief, and undergo a kind of death in its capacity to feel, in order to survive and live on. In this sense, the 'formal feeling', which numbs the person, is a kind of rescue. It is as if the ceremony helps to cope with the grief, as perhaps the poem does, so that the speaker is able to continue. [*AO1, for making an interpretation of the speaker's state of mind, and of the 'message' of the poem.*]
- Dickinson writes that 'feet, mechanical, / go round – / a wooden way', and while these lines makes

movement seem dreary, like a spinning wheel or some other dull work, the feet continue to trudge onwards. The line about the feet is broken up by punctuation, as if to really emphasise the trudging onward. [*AO1 for making the point about the feet trudging on, but also AO2 for talking about the caesura.*]

- At this point in the poem, the rhymes temporarily stop, as if it does not matter which word follows what, just as it does not matter if the path that is trod is 'ground or air or ought'. [*AO2 for talking about form and structure and saying what effect they create and how they change the meaning.*]
- The very abstract image of 'a quartz contentment, like a stone' seems at first to be redundant. If it is quartz it is not just like a stone, but is in fact a stone. Yet Dickinson's speaker says this for several reasons. The first is that in that repetition, the stoniness is emphasised, and the second is that it returns us to the rhyme. The formality, in the sense of 'poetic form', hardens the speaker. This is numbness, but it is also like quartz crystal. It is not just any stone, but a stone that shines. It is a hard-won contentment, even if it feels cold. [*AO2 for talking about how language, form and structure create meaning.*]

Theme/Paragraph Three: Dickinson continues the confusion between death and life in the third stanza.

- The phrase 'the hour of lead' again emphasises the heaviness of the experience of grief. However, this heaviness, which is likened to that of a metal ('lead'), is linked to the word 'outlived' through the *aabb* rhyme scheme established in the first quatrain (though 'lead' and 'outlived' do not in fact quite rhyme). You would normally only say that you can outlive living things, and this use here helps to suggest that the grief itself, and the experience of it, is alive. [*AO1 for making an interpretation. I have supported it with a quotation but also analysed that quotation in formal terms, so it should score something for AO2.*]

- The final simile, where a comparison is made between the pain grief induces and the way 'Freezing persons / recollect the snow', is extremely complicated. It is saying, I think, that we remember the painful hour of grief in the way that a person who is being frozen to death remembers being frozen. First, we feel cold and then numb, and then we finally feel nothing. But this grief, and the death-like sensation it induces, is also something we eventually outlive. The poem, layering paradox upon paradox, seems to imply that when we let go of this grief – a grief that is in a sense alive, but which feels like dying – we experience yet another form of death. [*This point should cover both AO1 and AO2, as I have talked about a simile, which is a technical feature, but really I am offering an interpretation of the ideas in the poem.*]
- Perhaps Dickinson is talking about the struggle to hold something in mind. When you lose a person, even getting over them may feel like a loss. You struggle even against losing the grief. [*AO1 for offering an interpretation that clarifies the point made in the analysis above.*]
- The dashes which create caesuras in the final line seem to suggest not just divided stages of grief but the way that things are lost piece by piece. Then the final

phrase, 'then the letting go', which is longer, mirrors the letting go itself. In this way, Dickinson suggests that the experience of grief totally transforms you to the point where the pain becomes a thing that you hold on to in order not to lose the person that you are grieving for. [*AO2: what I have tried to do here is make a comparison between the way time is controlled by the formal features of the poem, and the way in which the events of the poem unfold. What you're trying to discover is whether some of the features the poet uses create patterns that mirror the story of the poem. If it is about someone getting old and weaker and the lines get shorter, that might do the trick, for example.*]

Conclusion

For my conclusion, as ever, I'm going to offer a summary, but am going to try to make an additional point, as a twist. This one is about the shape of snowflakes, and may seem slightly odd, but showing an imaginative response to the poem is part of understanding it. You want to try to stretch your mind around a poem and pick up on the details that spark your imagination. You can bring some of that response into an essay.

> "Dickinson's poem suggests that the experience of grief is so intense that it takes on strange shapes. The only way to survive grief is to lose important aspects of one's self, and yet when the grief finally goes, that is another loss. As the poem's 'feet, mechanical, go round', we are given a vision of a cycle of death and rebirth in which the poem itself, as a 'formal' feeling, serves to give shape to what would otherwise be a

blankness, like the snow. Attending to the form of one's feelings thus becomes both a way of distracting yourself from your own pain and doing justice to the grief that caused that pain. Each snowflake has a shape, which we do not see when we think about the whiteness of the snow. However, looked at closely enough, the snow looks like crystal. Dickinson suggests that looking this closely might help us deal with the cold."

An 1847 daguerreotype of Emily Dickinson.

COMPARATIVE MINI ESSAY

EMILY BRONTË'S 'TO A WREATH OF SNOW'

To A Wreath of Snow

Emily Brontë

O transient voyager of heaven!
O silent sign of winter skies!
What adverse wind thy sail has driven
To dungeons where a prisoner lies?

Methinks the hands that shut the sun
So sternly from this morning's brow
Might still their rebel task have done
And checked a thing so frail as thou.

They would have done it had they known
The talisman that dwelt in thee,
For all the suns that ever shone
Have never been so kind to me!

For many a week and many a day
My heart was weighed with sinking gloom

When morning rose in mourning grey
And faintly lit my prison room.

But angel like, when I awoke,
Thy silvery form, so soft and fair,
Shining through darkness, sweetly spoke
Of cloudy skies and mountains bare;

* transient – temporary.
* checked – blocked.
* talisman — a sacred object symbolising something else.

Q2. In both 'After Great Pain' and 'To a Wreath of Snow', the speakers use the image of the snow as a way of thinking about grief. What similarities or differences are there in the way they present this feeling?

[8 marks]

Mini Introduction

Here, I offer my summary of what the two poems share in terms of subject and perspective. I have also summarised how I think their perspectives differ.

> "In both 'After Great Pain' and 'To a Wreath of Snow', snow offers the speakers a consolation. However, the ways that it offers that consolation are very different in the two poems. In Dickinson's piece, the snow is a symbol of freezing and numbing, and perhaps most

useful as a reminder that the pain will pass, either by melting as snow will, or by killing you. In the Brontë poem, however, the snow comes to remind a 'prisoner' of the outside world. It suggests brightness even in its coldness."

Mini Paragraph One

Here I talk about how the second poem uses language to create its perspective.

- Whether this prison is a literal prison, or simply a prison of profound grief, the snow works against the prison in Brontë's poem because it suggests an open space. In the first two lines it is associated with 'heaven' and 'winter skies'. It is not the ground that it touches that the snow reminds the speaker of, nor its cold, but its origin in the sky. The poet uses an extended metaphor where the clouds become hands which 'stop the sun / so sternly from the morning's brow', but even though the clouds can prevent the sun from shining, they cannot stop the snow from falling. The fact that these clouds are personified as part of the body helps to suggest that the grief is a kind of depression or sadness: not so much a physical prison, but a prison of the mind.
- The pun where 'morning rose in mourning grey', shows something of the same kind of personification, where the weather is connected to the mind's sadness. The snow, instead of this dull grey of sadness, is a 'talisman' of something special. Unlike the ordinary, everyday sun, it seems novel. The speaker tells us that

'all the suns that ever shone/ Have never been so kind to me!' as if her days have been hard, so this extra moment seems different.

Mini Paragraph Two

Here I discuss the key difference in terms of how the poems present their subject.

- This is a bit like the 'mechanical' existence of the speaker who has experienced great pain in Dickinson's poem. The sun goes round in a 'mechanical' way, like the feet, and this has turned the room into a prison. Both poems have an image of brightness — quartz, in the case of Dickinson, and 'silvery' snow in the case of Brontë — as ways of taking comfort, but Dickinson's is much more ambivalent. The bright object of Dickinson's poem is hard, like a stone, whereas Brontë pointedly makes note of the softness of the snow. For Brontë, the snow is out of the ordinary, whereas Dickinson uses it as a metaphor not for the out of the ordinary moment, but the numbness that comes after. It seems clear that Brontë's speaker is not 'freezing' and losing herself. Perhaps this resilience can best be seen in the difference between the 'hands' that Brontë describes and the 'feet' in Dickinson's poem. Brontë's hands have a purpose, a 'rebel task', and thus even her speaker's opponents seem to be part of the human world. For Brontë, grief can take away much but not the self.

Mini Conclusion

Finally, I try to make a brief general point, which sums up the difference between the poems.

"The softness and otherworldliness of Brontë's snow, reminding her of a place to which she might escape, is very different from the cold oppressiveness of Dickinson's snow. However, for both poets, there is something crucial about the way they stress that the snow is 'transient'. Dickinson says that we will let go of grief, and the snow, unlike the sun, does not regularly repeat itself. It is a sign that things pass, even sadness."

A statue of Emily Brontë in Bradford. Copyright © Tim Green.

PAPER EIGHT: POEMS ON ELSEWHERE

ESSAY PLAN: CLAUDE MCKAY'S 'THE TROPICS IN NEW YORK'

The Tropics in New York
Claude McKay

Bananas ripe and green, and ginger-root,
    Cocoa in pods and alligator pears,
And tangerines and mangoes and grape fruit,
    Fit for the highest prize at parish fairs,

Set in the window, bringing memories
    Of fruit-trees laden by low-singing rills,
And dewy dawns, and mystical blue skies
    In benediction over nun-like hills.

My eyes grew dim, and I could no more gaze;
    A wave of longing through my body swept,
And, hungry for the old, familiar ways,
    I turned aside and bowed my head and wept.

* alligator pear – an avocado.
* rills – a kind of stream.

Q1. In 'The Tropics in New York', how does Claude McKay present the speaker's memory of the tropics?

[24 marks]

Before we dive in...

Claude McKay was a Jamaican poet who moved to the USA. Here, he takes a moment to reflect on his own homeland and heritage. This is a perennial theme in poetry, which has so often been written by exiles, migrants and wanderers, and so let's have a look at how McKay manages to wring some poetic juice out of a bunch of fruit he looked at in a shop window.

Introduction

As ever, I'm going to offer a brief summary: this time, of what the speaker's memories **are like.** By this I mean how they make him feel. We know a bit about what the memories are, but the essay needs to say what it is about them that makes them move the speaker.

> "In 'The Tropics in New York', Claude McKay presents the speaker's memory of the tropics as overpowering his present experience. Though his memory is triggered by seeing fruits and other foods in what is presumably a store, he makes it clear that the tropics he is talking about are an inescapable part of his identity, something that he carries with him. The poem

suggests not merely that he remembers the tropical fruit that he sees in the stall, but that the way he behaves, even when he weeps, is in some way tropical."

Theme/Paragraph One: At first, the speaker's memories of the tropics are at a remove. He is reminded of them by the fruit, rather than by any thought of his own.

- The poem introduces the speaker's memories by using the fruit metonymically.[1] We are simply given exotic seeming fruits which are associated with Caribbean food culture. [*This is an AO2 point, because it is about the ways metonymy works in the poem. The fruit stands in for the tropics, and the glass stands in for the present urban life that divides McKay from this fruit. There it is, just out of reach.*]
- However, the rhyme words bring certain ideas to prominence in the first stanza. 'Root' and 'fruit' serve as reminders of the ways that food grows out of the soil into something. It has roots and it develops. As the speaker notices these fruits, it seems that the poet is comparing the speaker himself to a fruit: something that has sprung from a particular root, which is the tropics. [*AO2 for talking about language, form and structure.*]
- The fruit is behind glass in New York, far from its point of origin, and this is the same for the speaker. He describes the fruit as 'set in the window, bringing memories', and it is memories that connect both

speaker and fruit to the tropics. [*AO1 for making an interpretative point, backed up by a quotation.*]

Theme/Paragraph Two: The speaker therefore connects his own roots to the fruit in the subsequent stanzas, remembering the landscape where the fruit comes from.

- Here the language becomes more 'poetic' — more florid and full of adjectives — as the speaker begins to describe the Caribbean landscape. The poet writes of 'fruit-trees laden by low-singing rills / and dewy dawns and mystical blues skies'. The previous stanza had simply described the fruit. The only adjectives were 'ripe', 'green' and 'fit'. Now, the fruit is reconnected to the source and comes alive. [*AO2 for describing how the language creates meaning.*]
- Here, the alliteration of 'dewy dawns' is perhaps the most obviously exaggerated moment, but the whole tone seems more alive, as if something has awoken in the speaker. His memories make the whole landscape seem holy, which may be why the hills are described as nun-like. [AO2, AO1. *The phrase 'nun-like' is perhaps the weirdest in the whole poem. I have here offered an interpretation of them as nun-like simply because they receive the blessing, but there seems to be more to it than that. Maybe it's worth thinking about the shape of nuns in their black habits and the hills of Jamaica at Dawn. Perhaps the similarities are there. Whenever you find something like this in a poem, it's worth making a note to think: why might it be there? Have a go at offering an explanation — that's the point of an exploratory interpretation. Try to think with all of*

your senses about any associations a word has. An argument can be like a scalpel because it is precise. A moustache can be like a scalpel because it shares its shape. But maybe it's also a very precise moustache.]

Theme/Paragraph Three. In the third stanza, however, the speaker realises that he is cut off from this source of life, and his memories make him melancholy.

- At this point the liveliness of the language declines. Every word in this stanza is a monosyllable, which suggests a kind of regularity or even monotony and marks a stark contrast to the previous stanza. There, everything was flowing, whereas here each word is a self-contained unit, slightly disconnected, a bit like the fruit he is looking at. [*AO2 for describing how the language is used to create meaning.*]
- The use of the word 'hungry' at this point allows for a particularly powerful irony. The fruit has made him hungry for something that the fruit itself cannot provide. McKay could presumably easily go into the store and buy a mango, but he cannot get the 'old ways' back. [*AO1 for making an interpretation of the events of the poem. When you describe the speaker and what he or she might want to do, you are generally in AO1 territory.*

Conclusion

I had an idea that I wanted to put in the previous paragraph, but I think it's better if you have a really good idea that adds a twist to save it for the conclusion. If you don't have one, you can still get good marks with a simple summing up of your point, but try to add a twist if you can.

> "In spite of this disconnection, the final image of weeping is itself a tropical one. McKay uses the image of a wave of longing, which reconnects him to the natural landscape that he was describing in the second stanza. When he bursts into tears, here, there is a forcefulness which makes his tears not seem like any rain, but rather to have the force of a tropical storm. The word 'tropical' often indicates more liveliness and passion. The passion that the speaker expresses here, in weeping over the fruit, seems to be the real tropics. More than the fruit, he himself, even in a society whose new ways might constrain him, brings the tropics to New York."

COMPARATIVE MINI ESSAY

W. B. YEATS'S 'THE LAKE ISLE OF INNISFREE'

The Lake Isle of Innisfree
W. B. Yeats

I will arise and go now, and go to Innisfree,
And a small cabin build there, of clay and wattles
made;
Nine bean-rows will I have there, a hive for the
honey-bee,
And live alone in the bee-loud glade.

And I shall have some peace there, for peace comes
dropping slow,
Dropping from the veils of the morning to where the
cricket sings;
There midnight's all a glimmer, and noon a purple
glow,
And evening full of the linnet's wings.

I will arise and go now, for always night and day

I hear lake water lapping with low sounds by the shore;
While I stand on the roadway, or on the pavements
grey,
I hear it in the deep heart's core.

Q2. In both poems, the speakers describe their longing to be somewhere else. What are the similarities and/or differences between the ways the poets present these longings?

[8 marks]

Mini Introduction

Here, I offer my summary of what the two poems share in terms of subject and perspective. I have also summarised how I think their perspectives differ.

> "In both poems, Yeats and McKay present speakers whose minds wander to distant places, and who both carry those places with them in a way that changes how they see the cities they are in. When, as Yeats puts it, they stand on 'the pavements grey', they are driven to seek out this purer world."

Mini Paragraph One

Here I talk about how the second poem uses language to create its perspective, and compare it briefly to the first poem.

- The two poems both use a three-stanza structure to create a similar narrative, but while Mckay's moves from the present to the past and back again, Yeats's poem is more cyclical. He begins both the first and final stanzas with 'I will arise and go now'. The repetition makes it seem as if the whole poem takes place in its nostalgic elsewhere. [*nostalgia is the ancient Greek word for homesickness, and is a useful one to remember.*] There is no obvious change between Yeats's second and third stanzas. One could read his active assertion as very different from McKay's speaker. McKay does not even mention himself or his speaker until the third stanza. The memories that the fruits bring are not brought to him, they are simply brought. McKay a first seems more passive in the face of his memories, while Yeats declares that he will 'arise' and go to them.

Mini Paragraph Two

- However, Yeats's vision of going and building might be less active than it seems. If saying 'I will arise and go now' once seems decisive, saying it twice has a bit more of the air of someone repeating 'I really shouldn't' as they help themselves to a third piece of cake. Even though Yeats describes in detail exactly how many bean rows he will have, his plan seems to belong to a kind of permanent future. The 'nine bean rows' seem to be chosen because nine sounds good next to bean. It is as if the fantasy of beauty itself is most important. A 'bee-loud glade' could be scary if it was not described in such a pretty way. Yeats says that

'always night and day' he hears the lapping of the lake-water, but that 'always' seems to imply that he has not done anything about his desire to go so far. It is as if the Innisfree that he goes to is an Innisfree of the mind. He has gone now, and he goes all the time to this island of the imagination.
- This is perhaps why both poems use the same structure of interlocking rhymes: to suggest moving away and coming back, as one experiences the pull between the present and the past. This is what the two poems share, which is their sense that the poem can bind different experiences together.

Mini Conclusion

Finally, I try to make a brief general point; but for this last one, I thought I'd spice things up by focusing on a similarity. The two poems have many differences, but it is this idea of what the imagination can do that I want to end with. This is one of the most wonderful things we can get from reading a poem: a sense that everything is slightly changed by seeing a new connection between the world outside and our own inner lives. It's that shock of recognition, the moment when you hear a phrase like 'the bird's fire fangled feathers dangle down', and the sounds and the shapes and the meaning seem to overlap, and promise that what we experience is not just endless separate things, but a shape and a pattern: a way of holding our lives together.

> "In this way Yeats is more like McKay, whose tropics are inside him, than he is different: they both speak of what Yeats calls the 'deep heart's core'. When the outside world does not quite live up to their memories,

they call on the faculty of the imagination to compensate them: to show them ways to connect their past and present, and to remind them that they have not lost the things they wanted to hold on to."

A statue of W. B. Yeats in Sligo, Ireland.
Copyright © Marcus Murphy.

ENDNOTES

Essay Plan: Christina Rossetti's 'In an Artist's Studio'

1. **Iambic Pentameter** is a when every line has ten syllables where a **stress** falls on every second syllable. Think *Be**cause** Be**cause** Be**cause** Be**cause** Be**cause***. Stress is complicated, but think about how you talk when you speak. Certain syllables are emphasised.

Most of the time, when you say **Lon**don, for example, the stress falls on the first syllable – whereas, when you say pur**sue**, the stress will fall on the second. You might stress some syllables more than others for emphasis, but most words have a natural place where the stress falls. Words with one syllable will have a stress if you say them by themselves. But if you say any two syllables together you will naturally stress one more than the other. 'The **truth**', for example, will be pronounced by most people with the stress on truth. If a word has more than two syllables, it could have one or two (or more) stresses. **Com**pe**tit**ion, for example.

Traditional metred poetry makes a music from organising words so that the stress falls in set patterns. Aside from iambic pentameter (5 stresses) the most common metre is iambic tetramer (4 stresses). If you want to learn how to do this, practice thinking about where the stress falls in a range of words. Say, **Build**ing. Gir**affe**. Cellar? Convert? Reading? Sympathy? Turban? Combinatorial? Cinema?

2. **Caesura.** A pause in a line. Normally this is done by punctuation. Here is an example from Percy Shelley's 'Ode to the West Wind':

> Yellow, and black, and pale, and hectic red,
> Pestilence-stricken multitudes: O thou,
> Who chariotest to their dark wintry bed

As you read each line, you can see that the punctuation makes you pause between 'Yellow', and 'black', and 'pale', and 'hectic red'. The flow is interrupted, just as it is between 'pestilence stricken multitudes' and 'O thou'. On the other hand, the last line has no pauses in it, and so flows continuously. You can, if you like, think of the line break and the caesura working like two different kind of drums, say the bass and the kick. Together they create the rhythms.

3. **Enjamb**. To enjamb something is to make the sense run over the line break:

> I was happy
> yesterday

See how the line break changes how we experience that happiness? Or take this example, from John Milton's *Paradise Lost*

> from morn
> To noon he fell, from noon to dewy eve,

The fall is mirrored by the fall from line to line. Enjambment is a way to pause the meaning of a poem, to suspend it. Take John Keats's Endymion:

> A thing of beauty is a joy for ever:
> Its loveliness increases; it will never
> Pass into nothingness; but still will keep
> A bower quiet for us, and a sleep
> Full of sweet dreams, and health, and quiet breathing.

Each line after the first breaks in the middle of its meaning, so that idea of passing into nothingness is temporarily broken up, stopped or frozen by the poem. The line break creates a temporary space for hope that something might last.

Essay Plan: Katherine Philips's 'An Answer to Another Persuading a Lady to Marriage'

1. **Renaissance**. This is a period in European history named so because some people think it marks a cultural rebirth. It generally covers the 1400s and 1500s, though in England things started a little later and it's normally thought of as the 1500s to about 1642, when the English Civil War began.

Blazon. The blazon is a way poets have of describing people, often women, by describing them in parts. It takes its name the French word for a coat of arms, and it's a bit like describing a woman as if she were a shield with particular symbols on her face. An example from the Elizabethan poet Thomas Campion:

> Her eyes like angels watch them still,
> Her brows like bended bows do stand

Here's Shakespeare making fun of the tradition in his sonnets:

> My mistress' eyes are nothing like the sun;
> Coral is far more red than her lips' red.

Essay Plan: Edward Thomas's 'Adlestrop'

1. **Tetrameter.** See the note above. Tetrameter means that there are four stresses. Normally the rhythm will be iambic, as in the stress will be on every second syllable. But it could be Trochaic. That is when the stress is on the first syllable and then the third and so on. Here is an example from William Blake:

> **Ty**ger **Ty**ger, **burn**ing **bright**,

In the **for**ests **of** the **night**;

Blake actually cuts off the last unstressed syllable. This is called catalexis, but don't worry too much about that. The really technical stuff is not going to be that useful when you sit down to your exam. If you are fascinated by it, I suggest reading a book called *Poetic Rhythm* by Derek Attridge.

2. **Connotations.** A statement is normally thought to have both denotations, what it means, and connotations. A connotation is sort of like the extra meaning that comes along with the intended meaning. Here's an example from a poem by Andrew Marvell:

My vegetable love should grow
Vaster than empires and more slow

Here the poet is saying that, like a vegetable, his love will grow slowly. But that is just the denotation. The connotation is the other associations we have with the word vegetable. Vegetable love sounds a bit funny doesn't it? It connotes being green, without a brain, good for you but maybe a bit less tasty than carbs or junk food. These connotations are sometimes an intentional part of the poem, and sometimes an accident, but if a poet is saying 'I am caught in your net of love', you might want to think why the poet has decided she wants the connotations that come with that, such as her being a fish.

Essay Plan: Andrew Marvell's 'The Mower to the Glow Worms'

1. **Alliteration**. The placement of particular patterns of consecutive consonants at the start of a word. In the first poetry written in English – that is, from before the Norman Conquest – alliteration was used all the time. Alliteration as a regular structuring device continued, as in this poem from the 14th century: Sir Gawain and the Green Knight. Don't worry about what it says, just look at the pattern:

SIÞEN þe sege and þe assaut watz sesed at Troye,
Þe borȝ brittened and brent to brondeȝ and askez,

See all those 's' and 'b' words? But what purpose does alliteration serve? Well it draws your attention to the language, or intensifies. It's sort of like when all the colours match in a film. It makes things look slightly articifial. Some poets even make fun of it. Here's William Wordsworth:

> I have lengthened out
> With fond and feeble tongue a tedious tale.

So when you see alliteration, think about repetition and similarity. Why does the poet want us to see things as similar. This is not that dissimilar to consonance and assonance, but alliteration is more noticeable, and perhaps clunkier.

2. **Pathetic Fallacy.** This is when the weather or landscape are a mirror for the feelings of the poet. There is a much more complicated history of argument around this term, but all you need to know is that's how we currently tend to use it. If it rains when people are sad, that's pathetic fallacy. Here's a little bit of Thomas Hardy doing it:

> I leant upon a coppice gate
> When Frost was spectre-grey,
> And Winter's dregs made desolate
> The weakening eye of day.

The winter is not just out there in the world. It's how Hardy feels, too. The frost is 'spectre-grey', and Hardy is thinking about death.

Comparative Mini Essay: Lord Tennyson's *The Princess*

1. **anaphora.** This is a Greek word that we tend to use to mean repetition. If your poem has an otherwise loose structure, this can help give it shape. Here's the eighteenth-century poet Christopher Smart doing it in Jubilate Agno:

> For I will consider my Cat Jeoffry.

For he is the servant of the Living God duly and daily serving him.
For at the first glance of the glory of God in the East he worships in his way.
For this is done by wreathing his body seven times round with elegant quickness.
For then he leaps up to catch the musk, which is the blessing of God upon his
prayer.
For he rolls upon prank to work it in.
For having done duty and received blessing he begins to consider himself.
For this he performs in ten degrees.
For first he looks upon his forepaws to see if they are clean.

Here it creates a kind of musical structure, like the return of a chorus, but it can also be used to indicate being trapped in a routine, say, or a very precise approach to description. It can connect things together under a governing idea. Think about how Elizabeth Barrett Browning's Sonnet 43 works:

How do I love thee? Let me count the ways.
I love thee to the depth and breadth and height
My soul can reach, when feeling out of sight
For the ends of being and ideal grace.
I love thee to the level of every day's
Most quiet need, by sun and candle-light.
I love thee freely, as men strive for right.
I love thee purely, as they turn from praise.
I love thee with the passion put to use
In my old griefs, and with my childhood's faith.

Here the repetition of 'I love' groups many very disparate concepts, the depths of the soul and the quiet memories. Everything, it seems, is changed by love.

2. **quatrain.** A quatrain is a stanza made of four lines.

3. **assonance.** Assonance is the repetition of a vowel sound. Just like I did there in V**ow**el S**ou**nd. Now how do you use that in a poem? Again it can create certain kinds of repetition

effects, or can be used to create an almost rhyme. In modern pop music assonance counts as full rhyme, whereas in poetry it tends to be treated as something different.

Essay Plan: Arthur Hugh Clough's 'Say Not the Struggle Nought Availeth'

1. **Syntax.** Syntax is the structure of your sentence, the way it is ordered. You can change the way we experience a sentence by putting the words in a different order. By putting the words in a different order, you can change the way we experience a sentence. A poet can try to use long or short sentences, and differing numbers of clauses, to control your experience of time. Look at this bit of a poem, William Wordsworth's long autobiographical epic, The Prelude:

> O'er paths and fields
> In all that neighbourhood, through narrow lanes
> Of eglantine, and through the shady woods,
> And o'er the Border Beacon, and the waste
> Of naked pools, and common crags that lay
> Exposed on the bare fell, were scattered love,
> The spirit of pleasure, and youth's golden gleam.

The sentence structure is extremely complicated, but as we read it, particularly as it plays against the line break, the syntax means that we experience the things the poet describes in a very particular order. We see the search across the landscape before we reach the objects, 'scattered love'.

2. **Consonance.** This is the repetition of consonants. Not at the beginning of a word, that would be alliteration, but inside them. Skittish cattle, for example. Again this can be used for many effects, but you want to think to yourself: why is the poet drawing my attention to repetition. Sometimes this is just because it sounds nice, but even that creates an effect on you.

Comparative Mini Essay: 'Childe Harold's Pilgrimage' by Lord Byron

1. **Short 'I' Sound.** Most vowels have long and short forms when written down. "Down" has the long O sound whereas "Pond" has the short one. A line of poetry that only had short vowels, like 'To sit and think of ponds in winter' has a slightly different feel from 'to Lie by open fields and flower strewn groves'.

Essay Plan: Claude McKay's 'The Tropics in New York'

1. **Metonym** Metonymy is when an object or concept stands in for a larger concept that it is associated with. If you hear someone refer to a businessman as a suit, or the Queen as 'the crown', these are kinds of metonymy. Technically these examples come very close to being synecdoche, but stop short of where most people draw that slightly fuzzy line line. Think of it like this: a synecdoche is a part standing in for a whole. 'All hands on deck' is a demand that the sailors and not just their hands come onto the deck. Metonymy is the broader process of connection; the football team is called England, because it is connected to England, The top brass (the generals) of the army are called that because they used to have a brass plaque on their military hats. Is this a part or a connected idea? It's ambiguous. Americans sometimes refer to the statue of liberty, Lady Liberty, when they want to talk about the idea of liberty itself, that would be more clearly metonymic without synechdoche. Another example of metonymy that is clearly not synecdoche would be referring to the Prime Minister as 10 Downing Street. The workings of a poem are often metonymic; a budding flower carries with it the association of spring, and that first image will stand in for the theme that the poem then develops.

Printed in Great Britain
by Amazon

72c65f9b-ff0a-492c-b4d4-bcd6a3d313ccR02